KIERKEGAARD'S EXISTENTIALISM

KIERKEGAARD'S EXISTENTIALISM

The Theological Self and the Existential Self

George Leone, Ph.D., Th.D.

KIERKEGAARD'S EXISTENTIALISM
THE THEOLOGICAL SELF AND
THE EXISTENTIAL SELF

iUniverse books may be ordered through booksellers or by contacting:

iUniverse LLC
1663 Liberty Drive
Bloomington, IN 47403
www.iuniverse.com
1-800-Authors (1-800-288-4677)

ISBN: 978-1-4917-4361-4 (sc)
ISBN: 978-1-4917-4360-7 (e)

Library of Congress Control Number: 2014915150

Printed in the United States of America.

iUniverse rev. date: 11/11/2014

Acknowledgment

As I was writing this book I would, from time to time, think of Sally, the only other person I've ever known who had an appreciation of Kierkegaard. When we were attending college at Memphis State University, we would frequently meet in her studio, listen to the Rolling Stones, and discuss Kierkegaard while she painted. These discussions we had helped deepen my own appreciation of Kierkegaard when I came upon him again in the existential course of my undergraduate studies in philosophy. It was these discussions that established in me a lifelong desire to write this book.

Contents

Introduction

When Soren Kierkegaard died in 1855, he had already gathered around him something of a following throughout his native Denmark. By then he had written approximately twenty volumes of books, including several collections of "edifying discourses." Those who were attracted to him were apparently drawn to the religious nature of much of his work, and paradoxically he was claimed by both liberal and conservative Christians as their immediate forefather. Within twenty-five years of his death, Kierkegaard began to be translated to the rest of Europe (Lowrie 1970).

The interest in his work for European philosophers was basically its theological tone. But for them there was an added dimension that was beginning to be felt in philosophy. It was the phenomenological development of Edmund Husserl (1859–1938). This was a philosophical approach that attempted to arrive at a clear perception and understanding of reality by turning to the basis of all knowing, namely the conscious subject. Since the subjective reflectively-conscious self was the focus of all of Kierkegaard's writings, Husserl was greatly influenced by him. From Husserl, both Martin Heidegger (1889–1976) and Jean-Paul Sartre (1905–1980) came under the spell of Kierkegaard and his emphasis on "this individual."

Thus it was that a significant and enduring interest in Kierkegaard arose in this country. Historically, the general culture of North America is steeped in the kind of individualism that even a cursory reading of Kierkegaard will reveal. It seems that in Kierkegaard we have a personification of our twentieth-century American experience, ranging from our excessive hubris of the interwar years to the nihilistic quagmire of Vietnam. We see in Kierkegaard the harbinger of the existential themes that we have struggled with in our four-hundred-year history, from our increasing crises of faith to our utter bankruptcy of moral values.

Kierkegaard's own struggles began when he broke off his engagement with Regine Olsen. In doing so, he deliberately let go of the last anchor he had in life that had kept him grounded and directed. He set himself adrift in the sea of life with nothing but his own inner sense of identity as "this individual" to serve as his compass. As "this individual," Kierkegaard took a stand in life that became known as "existential." The existential individual is one who has let go of, or in some way becomes detached from, one's social contexts and connections from which one has hitherto derived a sense of identity, direction, and purpose. The external circumstances and situations are no longer effective as a source for these aspects, and one has to find an inner source for all this.

Kierkegaard found two individuals in human history who became his role models, so to speak, to help him as he struggled with his self-chosen course in life. They each represented two different directions for the individual to go in. These two individuals were Socrates and Jesus, and they personified respectively the existential self and the theological self. On the one hand, Socrates was the individual who ultimately rested in his own wisdom, incomplete as it was. He was always testing others about their wisdom when they made claims to being able to teach it. This was especially poignant when he was sitting in his prison cell awaiting execution. He would not even listen to his friends when they tried to persuade him to escape from prison, but he constantly searched within himself to find the moral basis for his decisions. In this way, Socrates personified the true existential individual, who is responsible for his own decisions and actions based on those decisions.

On the other hand was Jesus, who likewise sought within himself for the basis of his choices. But he did not rest in his own wisdom, for he came out of a cultural tradition that looked to God for ultimate wisdom. Thus, Jesus took a stance in his relationship with God as the basis for his individual being, thereby surpassing Socrates, in Kierkegaard's mind. The personification of this form of wisdom was clearly present when Jesus was, as Socrates was, facing death. Then he rested in his relationship with God to justify his choices and to redeem the meaning of his life. Because Jesus took this stance, he became the personification for Kierkegaard of the theological self.

In this book I will describe what it means to become a self as described in the life and writings of the individual Soren Kierkegaard. Of all the philosophers in the vast and varied history of philosophy, Kierkegaard alone concentrated on describing how it was that one became a self. He did not call himself a psychologist, however. He identified himself more as a combination of poet and philosopher, though not a philosopher in the sense of the system builders, such as Kant and Hegel, who preceded him. Kierkegaard's sole purpose in life was to become a true individual. The true individual is that person who has become a real self. Moreover, Kierkegaard sought to lay out this process in writing for others to have a road map, so to speak, to help them in embarking on this journey for themselves. There was always the caveat, however, "if one wants to." Thus, for Kierkegaard the thoughts expressed in his writings were the expression, or experience, of being a self.

Kierkegaard did not write objectively or scientifically about the process of becoming a self. Rather, his voluminous writing was itself the expression and manifestation of the process of becoming a self as it occurred in and as the life of Kierkegaard. Thus, Kierkegaard did not so much describe this process as he did exemplify it in his writing and living, his thought and experience. It is the unity of the two that makes him the true father of existentialism. This is the reference of "Existential" in the title.

What Kierkegaard uncovered through this process was the fact that becoming a self is not so much a psychological event as it is a spiritual one. As a psychological development, the self is achieved in and through empirical standards. That is, psychologically understood, the self becomes a self through a fundamental relationship that an individual has with the world. The "seedling self," so to speak, is a product of the world, but as long as this is all the self sees of itself, namely as being a product or expression of the world, it is not yet a true self. Thus, it is only in stepping out of the world in terms of using the world as its proof or standard of being that it is possible to become a real self.

When the self accomplishes this act, it enters its truth as a spiritual kind of being. That is, by definition that which is not identified with "the world" is not worldly, and that which is not worldly is what we call spiritual. The self manifests its truth as full self only as a spiritual kind of being. It becomes a purely subjective being insofar as it is not defined by any objective, or worldly, set of standards or proofs of its being. This standard, therefore, cannot be stated or defined objectively, because the standard is not "of the world," and only things of the world can be stated or defined objectively. Or, conversely, and more to the point, to define or state in an objective way a spiritual event is to paradoxically make that spiritual event into a thing of the world.

The "Theological Self" represents this attempt to explicate, describe, clarify, or identify this spiritual process of becoming a self through relating the self to the absolute. Kierkegaard discovered through his reflections the only standard or criterion by which the self can know itself as a true self. And in knowing its own criterion, the self becomes that which it is, namely a self. In other words, the criterion by which the self simultaneously knows that it is a self and actually becomes that self must and can only be a criterion that is like itself. For, the self's existence and consciousness of itself occur in the same moment, thus revealing the true nature of the self as spiritual. There is only one spiritual reality that has this same aspect in which knowing itself *is* its existence, making it thereby the absolute, and that is what we call God.

But we shall see that what Kierkegaard calls God is not the same as what, for example, Spinoza meant. For Kierkegaard, God is the eternal aspect of the self, but It is not a preexisting reality that creates the self as a mechanistic model of the world would have it. Rather, as it will become clear, Kierkegaard means to say that the self and God come into each other's presence in one and the same moment. Exactly what the paradox means is the explication of Kierkegaard's existential theology.

In part 2, the topic will be on how Socrates represented the first existential self. This is different from the theological self in that the existential takes as its criterion the awareness of standing apart from that which gave the self its identity. The theological self takes as its criterion the awareness of standing before and in relation to that from which the existential self separated. The existential self is not godless or atheistic. Rather, it accepts the reality that it exists as an individual, and it is in willingly existing as such and in choosing to exist as such that the existential self has its meaning.

PART 1
THE THEOLOGICAL SELF

Chapter 1

THE CHOICE

Early in his life, Kierkegaard became vaguely aware of a fundamental difference between merely believing something and truly knowing that which otherwise one might merely believe. This difference seemed to involve a further distinction between life lived only in segments and life lived fully. Beliefs, whether political, social, moral, or spiritual, inevitably lead to a life that is fragmented and lived in segments. This is because beliefs can never be more than partial in their impact on a person's life. To say, for example, "I believe that God is in his heaven and all is right with the world" has an impact only on my need for a sense of security in life. Such a belief does not reach into my actual lived experience that the world is often a tragic place.

More to the point for Kierkegaard was the Christian dogma that was prevalent in Copenhagen and throughout Denmark in general during Kierkegaard's lifetime of 1813–1855. This was the Lutheran form of Christianity into which Kierkegaard was born and in which he was steeped. Later in his life, toward the end in fact, he was to focus intently on what Luther represented and its effect on Christianity. But early in his life, Kierkegaard realized that merely believing or even understanding the meaning of Christianity was not enough if "it had no deeper significance" for him and his life (Dru 1958, 44). This thought was entered in Kierkegaard's journal on the first day of August 1835. That day was apparently full of insight for Kierkegaard, as suggested by several entries he wrote. He realized that "[T]he thing is to find a truth which is true *for me*, to find the idea for which I can live and die" (44). This idea "was what I lacked in order to be able to lead a complete human life and not merely one of understanding" (45). Kierkegaard did not want to base his life upon "something that is called objective—something that is in any case not my own" (45). Truth, as idea and as thought, had to permeate his entire being, for "[w]hat is truth but to live for an idea?" (45).

Mere knowledge was not sufficient for Kierkegaard. In drawing a parallel between knowledge and pleasure using a metaphor from the book of Genesis, he said, "I have tasted the fruit of the tree of knowledge, and often delighted in its taste. But the pleasure did not outlast the moment of understanding and left no profound mark upon me" (46). He stated that he has sought with resignation for the principle, the fundamental idea, of his life. He did not, however, find his self, "which was what I was looking for" (46). Kierkegaard followed this thought with another that goes to the heart of his life and thought. "One must know oneself before knowing anything else. It is only after a man has thus understood himself inwardly and has thus seen his way, that life acquires … significance" (46).

Kierkegaard, however, was aware that he was "still far from having reached so complete an understanding of myself"; however, out of a "profound respect for its significance, [I have] tried to preserve my individuality" (46–47). That is, Kierkegaard resisted the power of others' statements of what is true to pull him into their orb. He rather sought to master them, to study them individually and examine their importance in others' lives, "at the same time guard[ing] against going, like the moth, too near the flame" (47). The result of this effort was expressed in a profound statement in which Kierkegaard clearly made a choice.

> And so I stand once again at the point where I must begin my life in a different way. I shall now try to fix a calm gaze upon myself and begin to act in earnest; for only thus shall I be able, like a child calling itself "I" with its first conscious action, to call myself "I" in any deeper sense (47).

These reflections in Kierkegaard's journal have their precursors in certain incidents in Kierkegaard's life just after he entered the university to study theology in 1830. Kierkegaard was born into a strongly religious family immersed in Lutheran Christianity. As the last of seven children, he was doted upon, especially by his father. As a result, the two of them shared a deeply loving relationship. Yet it was a melancholic household, made so by a curious blend of the dark aspects of Lutheranism, on the one hand, and the basic fault of the father, on the other. Added to this was the death of Kierkegaard's mother and three siblings within three years of each other beginning in 1829 (Dru 1958).

The basic fault of Kierkegaard's father was a secret guilt that he had carried since childhood. Kierkegaard learned that his father had cursed God when he was only twelve years of age. The father's guilt and sense of sin weighed heavily upon him, and all his life he felt that God cursed him in return. This created in Kierkegaard's father a melancholic personality that formed the emotional atmosphere in Kierkegaard's childhood.

In 1835, the same year as his insightful journal entries, but prior to them, leading up to them, Kierkegaard experienced what he called "The Great Earthquake" (Lowrie 1970, 68–76). He put it all together in his mind: his father's guilt, the loss of his mother and siblings, the melancholic darkness, the Lutheran doctrine of fundamental human sinfulness, and his father's strong desire and prompting for Kierkegaard to study theology (Collins, 1965). In his journal entry he saw that "[t]here must be a guilt upon the whole family, the punishment of God must be on it" (Dru 1958, 39). A year later, in 1836, he wrote, "[i]nwardly torn asunder ... I was, without any expectation of leading a happy earthly life ... without hope of a happy and comfortable future" (40). Two years later, in 1838, Kierkegaard's father died, and his imagination interpreted that loss as "the last sacrifice which he made to his love for me ... in order that if possible I might still turn into something" (60).

Though Kierkegaard had entered the university to study theology in 1830, he had been ambivalent about this course of study. He remained because his father wished it. Then, upon his father's death, Kierkegaard felt he owed it to him to finish the degree of doctor of theology. He envisioned himself as a pastor with a congregation and a family of his own (Capel 1964). In 1841 Kierkegaard finally completed his examination for the doctor of theology. Right after that, he became engaged to Regine Olsen and began working on his dissertation, *The Concept of Irony* (Kierkegaard, 1841/1989).

When Kierkegaard completed his theology degree, rather than feel that he had done this for himself, he saw that the last wish of his father was now fulfilled (Dru 1958). He felt that he was living his life according to his father's preferences for him, right down to the engagement with Regine. In Kierkegaard's days there was nothing more socially upright and laudable as to be a married pastor. But for Kierkegaard there was nothing more false and damaging to his integrity. Already in his dissertation he had presented Socrates as the image of a true individual, one who will not shape his life according to others' standards. Socrates always stood on his own two feet in "the infinite ... freedom of subjectivity" (*The Concept of Irony*, 211). Kierkegaard had too much of an inherent sense of integrity to allow himself to go any further with a falsely chosen life. He broke off the engagement with Regine, took Socrates as his model, and launched himself into who he really was. Stirred on by his inherited melancholy, a melancholy that he did not want to subject Regine to, he, as Socrates had in ancient times, sought a firmer ground for his life's happiness, while at the same time being, as was Socrates in his time, a gadfly. Where Socrates was a gadfly to the populace of Athens, Kierkegaard became the gadfly to the populace of the state-sponsored church, which he called Christendom.

Thus, the extensive statement of Kierkegaard, quoted earlier, expresses simultaneously the fact that he did not feel that his happiness lay in following any prescribed set of values, including those given by the church, *and* that therefore his work in life was to examine closely all that claimed objective validity as set standards for how to live life. Kierkegaard wanted above all to truly discover something that he could live and die for. His life's works, the many volumes of it, represented this attempt to work out what this was. He was to take nothing for granted, especially Christendom and its values, though he came to ultimately make a sharp distinction between Christianity and Christendom. The only thing given from which he could begin was not a thing at all, at least not as a given thing in the objective world. For, where Kierkegaard began, the one "thing" he could not help but to begin with was himself, the individual man.

Chapter 2

THE AESTHETIC AND THE ETHICAL

Kierkegaard began the two-volume work *Either/Or* (Kierkegaard 1843/1944), with a series of quips in which he encapsulates the polarity of human existence. He praises love and praises emptiness. He complains of meaninglessness and of fullness. He is full of contradictions in the opening pages of the first volume, the one that elucidates what it means to live for pleasure, the aesthetic life. In the second volume his concern is with what it means to live for duty, the ethical life. In this, his first major work, Kierkegaard holds before us two diverse ways of being.

The Aesthetic

If we live as Don Juan, we live for the pure eroticism of immediate life. If we live in immediacy, we live for the intensity of erotic, aesthetic arousal. One's whole self is centered on the quest for and conquest of the object of one's erotic desire. Pleasure is one's goal in life and one's meaning for living. The more intense the pleasure, the more one feels a meaning in life. Thus, the person who lives in immediacy is living for the emotional intensity that comes with the highest form of pleasure, the erotic. Also, the stronger the feeling or emotion, the more a person feels alive.

Kierkegaard distinguishes between three stages of the erotic. In the first stage, desire appears as only a vague possibility, almost as a dream, in which the object is presented as an enticement. The second stage is marked by desire beginning to seek for its object in the world. Desire in effect says that the erotic object is not just a dream. It is really possible that the desired object can be realized in actuality. Kierkegaard then says that the third stage is when desire becomes the action of desiring. This sounds like he is speaking of desire in the abstract. But what he means is that desire belongs to a person, a real self. It is the person's self that recognizes itself in both the act of desiring and in having the object before it as the symbol of what the self can be; that is, what the self is potentially (*Either/Or,* 1, 74–86).

When the object is still only the dream of possibility, the self sees it as the image of what it, the self, can be. The self does not yet have a firm grounding beyond the immediacy of life; that is, a grounding in itself. The self's grounding in immediacy is in the immediacy of desiring (*Either/Or,* 1, 95). This gives the self a hope, but since hope is the "yet to be realized," the hope is for what the self can be. However, since the self does not yet realize that it hopes for what it can be, the form this hope takes is as desire for an object which the self takes to be that through which it can become what it hopes to be. It sees itself, in other words, as a specific object that is already in the world.

This is the kind of dialectic that Kierkegaard envisages as leading from an impersonal desire to a personalized form of it and thence to the creation of a self through the object. This is the theme that is repeated throughout Kierkegaard's writings. The self seeks itself. Life is a quest to become the individual that one potentially is. The form of this quest begins naturally enough with a desire. However, though we begin with a desire for the self, this desire is always, first and foremost, a desire for that in which the self sees itself most clearly as a self. This desire is hope. This hope is to eventually become what one is, and this means what one is to become. Throughout Kierkegaard's writings, as throughout his life, one is not yet a full self, because one is always becoming that which one is potentially.

In the "Diary of the Seducer" of volume one of *Either/Or*, Johannes falls in love with the sole object of his desire, Cordelia. This is no doubt a poetic reconstruction of Kierkegaard's own love for Regine that he put aside, because he realized that, though one might become a self through love and marriage, nevertheless one is *not yet a self.* This realization of not yet being a self means that if one is not a self, then who is there who can really love the other, the object of one's desire?

Kierkegaard is the melancholic individual who realizes that whether one marries or not, one will regret it (*Either/Or*, 1, 37). He saw early on that whether he married Regine or not, there would be regret, because the melancholy that stayed with him throughout his life would always lead to regret. In his psychological insight, Kierkegaard knew that melancholy is not only regret for any choice he would make, but it is regret for living itself as long as living is centered in the object. In the first volume of *Either/Or*, climaxed in "The Seducer's Diary," Johannes's love for and quest after the love of Cordelia reflects the struggle of Kierkegaard to become a self knowing that, though the quest to fulfill the desire for the love of a woman is a strong and promising hope to become a full self through this love, he would not yet be a self upon the conquest of achieving the desire object, the love of Regine/Cordelia.

The Ethical

Kierkegaard pursues this growing awareness in the second volume of *Either/Or* as he reflects on his "predilection for … the first sensation of falling in love" (*Either/Or*, 2, 7). He recognizes that the object of the "first love" takes on an ideal and absolute quality in the mind of the lover, and at the same time he knows how deceptively seductive this process is. For, to pursue the first love as if it is the culmination of one's whole life, as if the end of life is in its beginning, and as if it is the nature of the self to give itself up to the first glimmer of itself, is a self-contradiction. The contradiction lies in the new desire that grows in the heart, a desire for the temporal and passing to be permanent and eternal. Indeed, the quality of the first love, the intensity of the first love, is such that it appears to propel the self directly into the eternal, so strong is its power. The deception lies in the fact that the only way the permanent and eternal can appear in the temporal and impermanent is if the first love is repeated endlessly, constantly recurring again and again. But this, of course, is impossible, and if a self becomes enraptured with the constant recurrence of its first love, then such a self has fallen into self-deception by taking the recollection of the first love as the actual initial experience of falling in love with the first love (*Either/Or*, 2, 144). Thus, in this way, no sooner does the self find itself in the beloved object than it loses itself in its attempt to make permanent that which is impermanent, thereby replacing the real object with a mere image in the recollection of the real.

Not only, then, does the self become obsessed with the first love and attempt to make it into the first and only and forever love, but it also takes this first discovery of itself that is reflected in the first love as its real self, as its truth. But, of course, the first love does not and cannot last, and the self experiences its first despair. Despair for Kierkegaard is the absence of all hope for the kind of absolute selfhood that is envisioned as attainable through the beloved (174). It needs to be remembered that for Kierkegaard the only goal of life, the sole goal for which he is called "the father of existentialism" (Lowrie 1970, 214), is the attainment of full selfhood. Despair is the loss of hope, not for attaining full selfhood, but for attaining it through the object of the first love.

When the self experiences despair for the first time, it is brought to an awareness of itself. Kierkegaard explains this by pointing out that when we lose the one thing that we have looked for to bring us to full selfhood, we despair over the world with a sense of utter disappointment. In fact, the self is made more aware of itself in despair of the world. The self realizes in despair that it cannot look to the things of the world for its coming into fullness. The self becomes poignantly aware of itself in being plunged into its lack. It still has itself, though not yet fully itself. That is, the self still has to become itself, though not through anything in the world. Thus it is that "in despair you have found yourself" (*Either/Or*, 2, 213). In allowing himself to experience the despair that comes from the ultimate and inevitable realization that the world of the first love, of the aesthetic pleasure seeking life, will never bring him to selfhood, Kierkegaard makes a choice. It is as if he has chosen despair. But he does not choose despair as a way of rejecting the world, for he is still in the world as it is. He rather chooses despair in order to come to himself. For, "when a man despairs he chooses again—and what is it he chooses? He chooses himself ... in his eternal validity" (215).

He chooses himself. What Kierkegaard means by this is that the self realizes itself as the absolute. He states, "in despair I choose the absolute, for I myself am the absolute" (217). The absolute is the self in its eternal validity. Kierkegaard speaks of the absolute in two ways. First, it is that beyond which nothing can be posited. The self is that which has no "beyond itself," for it is not, and can never be, posited as a thing in the world alongside other things. It is purely existential. When the self becomes aware of itself in the despair of ever finding itself in the object of its love and desire, it becomes aware that it can never be equated with any object that is in the world. It is not another thing in the world, therefore it cannot fully be itself when it seeks for itself through the desired object that it loves. In despair, the self realizes itself as *not a thing*, and therefore it is that beyond which nothing can be posited.

The second sense of the absolute for Kierkegaard is that in choosing the self in despair, one chooses the self absolutely. That is, one chooses only the self, for one cannot choose the object as self. The choice of self is not conditional. Kierkegaard does not say, "I will choose myself until I find another person to love. I will choose myself only to collect myself together until I find another to whom I will give myself." This is a false despair and a false choice. To make such a conditional choice is to make the self a thing in the world, but this leads to repeated despair until the self sees finally that it can only choose itself. This is to choose the self absolutely, finally, and resolutely. Thus, to bring both meanings of the absolute together, Kierkegaard says:

> But what is it I choose? Is it this thing or that? No, for I choose absolutely, and the absoluteness of my choice is expressed precisely by the fact that I have not chosen to choose this or that. I choose the absolute. And what is the absolute? It is myself in my eternal validity. Anything else but myself I never can choose as the absolute, for if I choose something else, I choose it as a finite thing and so do not choose it absolutely (218).

To choose the self, then, is the result of realizing that no *thing* in the world can ever be the self. This self that we choose is both abstract and concrete. Kierkegaard says that "[i]t is the most abstract of all things, and yet at the same time it is the most concrete—it is freedom" (218). The self is freedom. The very act of choosing is itself freedom. We cannot choose without being free to choose. Making a choice manifests the self as this freedom. In the act of choosing the self, that which is chosen, namely the self, comes into existence as freedom. A certain dialectical process is occurring. That which is chosen comes into existence with the choice, but that which is chosen already exists otherwise there could be no choosing. So in freedom I choose that which is freedom itself. Choosing the self is, therefore, the self as freedom choosing the self as absolute. In other words, "as a free spirit I am born of the principle of contradiction, or born by the fact that I choose myself" (220).

In choosing myself I do not transcend the world. I do not put aside my desire for the object of my love. I do not reject the world when I choose myself. I, rather, transform the world and its object that I desire in love. In choosing myself, I do not thereby abstract myself from the world, for I realize my inextricable connection with the world. I realize the vastness of this connection with the world. I am part of the world in historical time and in my social context. I am who I am because of the multifarious attributes that I am made up of, all of which connect me to the world in various ways. Thus, far from retreating from the world, I take up a stand in it.

Yet I am not part of the world, according to Kierkegaard, in a merely passive way. My connection to the world is not as depicted by the Romantic poets and mystics. For this would be to regress to the aesthetical, passively waiting for the effects upon myself of my encounters with the world. Rather, my connection with the world that is chosen when I choose myself is an active connection. I fight for possession of the world as it is represented by the object of my love. I cannot have the whole world but only that part of it which is that which I desire in love. Thus, the whole becomes represented by the single object of love. Since, however, I have chosen myself, my relation with the world in and through the single object of love becomes qualitatively different. For I no longer relate to the world as if it is my self.

Interlude

Here Kierkegaard makes a sudden shift. He points out that a person who has chosen the self cannot relinquish anything in the whole that is the world. In choosing the self, the person also chooses to acquire the world—that is, to take the world into himself in all its pain and hardship. This acquisition is expressed, he says, as repentance (*Either/Or*, 2, 220). It is with this sudden shift into the notion of "repentance" that Kierkegaard's thought incorporates and expresses many aspects of his life. For, it must be kept in mind that Kierkegaard is not building up any system of thought or philosophy of his own making. Nor is he only a spokesman or apologist for an already existing system, be it Hegelianism or Christianity. He is taking his existential immediacy as the beginning and end of his thinking. For Kierkegaard, the most urgent goal of his thinking is to become clear about his life (Dru 1958). All of his writings are one continuous attempt to work out this clarity, not of life in general, from the basis of some system or other, but of his individual life.

The connection, then, between choosing to be a self and realizing repentance is to be found in his earlier life. Kierkegaard realizes that in choosing to be a self he also unavoidably chooses the world that he came out of, the world that created him. That is, in choosing to be a self he realizes that he is not the author of himself. His root, that is, is that by which he is connected to the world (*Either/Or*, 2, 220). He comes out of the world, in other words, in the sense of being this particular individual. But this is not yet a self. Yet, it is as this particular individual who comes from the world that he tries to return to this source through aestheticism. In the form of erotic aestheticism he seeks (re)union with a woman, Regine. Lowrie (1970) suggested that there may be some connection between a mother who "counted for little" (24) in the household of Kierkegaard's early life and who died just as he left home for school, and his short-lived engagement to Regine some years later. In the form of tragic aestheticism, he experiences the futility of this hope for a repetition of what cannot be repeated.

Thus, when Kierkegaard chooses to be a self, he simultaneously relinquishes his desire for the "first love" (Regine? Mother?) and acquires the world through being absorbed in the root that eternally connects him to the world, the root that is the same object of his first love. Further, in choosing to be a self, he turns toward that which made him who he is, namely his father, with whom we have seen a very early identification. The quotation of a journal entry dated August 11, 1838, will make this more significant in the development of what emerges from Kierkegaard's inner turmoil. Part of this was quoted in the first chapter.

> My father died on Wednesday (the 9th) at 2 a.m. I had so very much wished that he might live a few years longer, and I look upon his death as the last sacrifice which he made to his love for me; for he did not die from me but *died for me* in order that if possible I might still turn into something. Of all that I have inherited from him, the recollection of him, his

transfigured portrait, not transfigured by the poetry of my imagination (for it did not require that) but explained by many an individual trait which I can now take account of—is dearest to me, and I will be careful to preserve it safely hidden from the world. He was a "faithful friend" (Dru 1958, 59–60).

The only way to account for Kierkegaard's inclusion of repentance in his choosing himself is to see it as the action of a guilty individual. He is guilty before God, because God has brought punishment upon the whole family. Therefore, "[t]here must be a guilt upon the whole family" (Dru 1958, 39). Kierkegaard has taken upon himself the "iniquity of the father which passed by inheritance to the son" (*Either/Or*, 2, 221). His deep identification with his father led Kierkegaard to take upon himself his father's guilt before God; therefore, when he chooses himself, he can choose only a self that is guilty. The only way to move forward as a self is to be a repentant self. "He repents back into himself, back into the family … until he finds himself in God" (220).

The Ethical Resumed

As a repentant self, Kierkegaard begins to reflect on his previous aesthetic lifestyle. In reflecting upon life, he enters the ethical life, a life of curbing the passions, of choosing to actively (that is, willingly and consciously) pursue a life in which self-fulfillment is found through self-negation. Where as an aesthete he was living passively for the effect of the world upon himself, an effect that can be both tragic and erotic, he has now turned toward an active ethically oriented life. The ethical does not consist in living according to some principle or standard, for this would be to again live aesthetically, since one would then live for the effect, in this case the effect of feeling righteous or saved. The ethical is, rather, the way of living in which one despairs of all hope for salvation as coming from the world. In despairing, one chooses to be in despair, and then finds that paradoxically "it is man's true salvation to despair" (*Either*/Or, 2, 225).

This only means, however, to despair of the saving effect coming from outside oneself. In reality, despair is the result of an active choice to relinquish the world as the source of oneself. The self, in choosing itself—that is, in choosing to become itself—chooses to live ethically, to choose itself absolutely. This is the ethical, "that whereby a man becomes what he becomes" (229). Kierkegaard no longer lives in the moment, for he lives reflectively. Reflection allows him to gain mastery over his lust for pleasure—that is, to no longer live in the moment, to no longer live passively waiting for the effect of the world to determine who he is. In living ethically, Kierkegaard lives "in possession of his self as posited by himself, that is, as chosen by himself, as free" (227). He therefore becomes what he becomes through freely choosing himself.

This ethical decision brings Kierkegaard to actively enter into a relationship in which the erotic feeling that was the main driving force of the aesthetic life is focused and refined into love. Love then becomes the impetus for the ethical life, and this leads Kierkegaard to the realization that marriage represents the highest expression of the ethical (151). For, where in the aesthetic life the self waits passively for the effect of the world upon it, whether pleasure (the erotic) or pain (the tragic), in the ethical life the self must actively engage through love with the beloved, giving itself to the beloved. To choose to be a self is exactly this choice to actively engage with the world through love in giving oneself to the beloved. Therefore, to choose to be a self leads, for Kierkegaard, to the paradox of choosing to give oneself to another. This is why marriage represents for Kierkegaard the highest expression of the ethical. For, the self in marriage has a duty to the beloved (149–51).

But if one is denied marriage in life, or if one chooses to not marry, then one must find another "object" to love and to which to give oneself. The only other possible "object" for Kierkegaard is God. In choosing the self absolutely, he chooses that beyond which there is nothing. Yet, at the same time he is choosing that which is not the cause of itself. Therefore, to choose the self necessarily involves the cause of itself, and the cause of the self, for Kierkegaard, is its eternal aspect. This is God. And since there is nothing beyond the self when it is chosen absolutely, then to choose the self is to choose God. This is not, however, to enter a mystical relationship with God. For, such a relationship would make of it an aesthetic relationship in which the self again passively enjoys the effect of the relationship. This is not the kind of relationship with God that Kierkegaard has in mind.

I will now turn to the next stage in the development of the self that Kierkegaard expressed both in his writings and in his life. He called this the religious stage, and it involves a specifically unique kind of relating with God. It is not mystical, nor is it devotional, both of which revert to the aesthetic. It is more like the relation that the Old Testament prophets had with God, in which God and self are separated by a vast abyss yet still try to speak to each other.

Chapter 3

THE RELIGIOUS STAGE

Kierkegaard introduces another way of experiencing the individual, and this is the individual as contrasted with the universal. The ethical is that position in which the individual posits himself as a self in its eternal aspect. This eternal aspect appears to the self as the universal. The universal defines the individual in terms of being that for which the individual lives. When the individual tries to express himself as individual rather than as the universal, or, better put, when the individual steps out of the universal, there is, for Kierkegaard, the origin of sin (*Fear and Trembling*, Kierkegaard, 1843/1980, 55). The individual can reconcile himself with the universal only by repenting and returning to the universal, which is to place his individuality again within the universal. This is the normal state of affairs for human existence and the source of most conflict in the individual. For, the impulse is for the individual to express and indulge himself as an individual in the world, actively seeking pleasure but in reality passively living for the effect that the world has on him. When the world fails the individual, as it inevitably will, the individual reacts with some form of indignation and sense of disappointment in the world for failing to live up to the individual's expectations and desires. When this disappointment causes the individual to reflect on himself, the person sees the real fault as lying within the failure to have truly chosen the self. The individual feels a vague sense of guilt; he repents, and, in turning back toward the self, relocates himself in a new relation with the universal, now seeing it as his source.

Kierkegaard says that if this is the ultimate that can be said of the human individual, then living ethically is the highest form of realization and the way to salvation (*Fear and Trembling*, 54). But clearly this is not the case, for the fact remains that the universal, after all, created this individual that Kierkegaard is and that all humans are. That is, the paradox of human existence is that each individual emerges as an expression of the universal in the world; but once in the world, each individual is faced with the choice of being a self, which includes the universal, or of being only the universal, which does not include the self. Put another way, as far as human existence is concerned, the universal design for human being is to know itself as individual being. The essence of human existence is in its concrete existing, and existing can be seen only as the individual. Yet, the paradox remains: the individual is itself the expression of the universal.

In our initial experiment with life, we live as individuals in pursuit of each our own pleasure in life. When we come to realize that pleasure and pain always come together, we take another look at our lives and at our purpose. Since we cannot avoid being individuals, we have to choose how we will live as individuals, either in pursuit of pleasure or by adjusting our individuality back into the universal, now in the form of ethical living. We believe that in choosing the ethical universal, we have chosen to be a self. But in reality the ethical leads to the relinquishing of the self, for while we may enter the universal out of reflection and repentance, and out of a profound disillusionment with the world, the turning toward the ethical is actually the attempt to save the self by immersion into the universal, returning to the source. This is an annulment of the self as individual and is an attempt to be the self as universal. But in doing this we have not in reality chosen to be a self. We do not truly choose the self until we choose it absolutely—that is, as the responsibility put upon us by the universal. It is this universal task to express the universal in and as each individual, to be an individual self.

Kierkegaard expresses all of this in *Fear and Trembling*. He says that the ethical is the universal and the highest form of it, as revealed by the dilemma that Abraham found himself in, being asked by God to sacrifice his son Isaac, is the love of the father for the son (59). Since the ethical is the universal, love is also the universal. The universal, however, is such because it is traceable back to God. God is the source of the universal, because the universal is divine (68). The ethical, insofar as it is a duty, is therefore a duty to God. Putting oneself in a relation to the ethical, however, is not to thereby enter a relation to God. For, the ethical comes from God but is directed toward "something external" (69). The individual is called upon as a duty to come out of interiority and express himself toward something. Kierkegaard says that he cannot love God as an object, because "God ... is understood as the divine—that is, the universal, that is, the duty" (68). We can, it seems, only obey this duty, accept this duty, but it makes no sense to say that we love this duty, for the duty itself is to love.

Kierkegaard also says that duty is "simply the expression for God's will" (60). Now it may happen, as it might have for Abraham, that adhering to the ethical may prevent us from doing God's will. What is emerging here is the situation that when we really listen to God's will, we may in fact have to step beyond the ethical. Since the ethical has its expression as "social morality" (55), and since God's will does not come in the same form as social morality—that is, as clearly defined rules—to truly follow God's will may actually appear as foolishness, immorality, or outright willfulness. We can only do God's will in some situations by developing a faith in our own actions that they are in fact God's will rather than a self-centered willful contradiction of God's will. Of course, killing is murder in ethical terms, but what Abraham was called upon to do was called sacrifice in religious terms (30).

When we lose a loved one, for example, because the beloved dies or rejects us, we say that the beloved has been taken from us. We erroneously say that this was God's will. We can as easily say that it was disease or the beloved's own act of will that took her from us. Kierkegaard implies that God's will is not something that comes from or is expressed by the world, since God's will is duty. Duty does not come from the world but rather comes from the ethical, the universal (248).

This is where faith is born. Faith is not a belief in God as a thing, however supreme and sublime, such as we have when we say, "I believe that there are good spirits and evil spirits." Nor is faith a belief in something that will happen, such as, "I will win her love in the end." True faith is, rather, the paradox that the single individual stands superior to the universal law (ethical, moral, or metaphysical) because when one chooses the self absolutely, one then "stands in an absolute relation to the absolute" (56). In other words, faith is not that all things happen by God's will or that all things work out for the best. Faith is not that God will give one's heart's desires to one who believes. This understanding of faith is simply disguised immediacy, lingering in mood, emotion, and passively waiting for the effect of the world upon oneself. True faith is that when we truly choose the self absolutely, we then relate ourselves absolutely to the absolute (70). Thus, when we lose our beloved, God's will becomes apparent only as we choose our self absolutely. We willingly accept our beloved's rejection of us, because we choose the self absolutely, and this puts us in an absolute relation with the absolute, God. We choose our basis in the self and not in the beloved. Our basis is God, because that is the basis of our self when we choose absolutely. Self and God are both chosen in the choice. They both come into existence with the choice when we absolutely choose the self. The choosing itself is the emergence into existence of both the self and God.

There is another dimension of this for Kierkegaard, and he makes a sharp distinction between having a kind of stoical resignation to events in one's life and having faith that in renouncing everything we gain it all back. This distinction seems to be drawn along the same line as the distinction between the world and the self. The so-called "knight of resignation" (50) resigns himself to the loss and even finds joy, peace, and rest in the pain of that loss (49). He has relinquished the world back to itself in a movement that gains for him "eternal consciousness in blessed harmony with … love for the eternal being" (48). Contrasted to the knight of resignation is the "knight of faith," who says, "By faith I do not renounce anything; on the contrary, by faith I receive everything" (48–49). He attains, paradoxically, the temporal "by virtue of the absurd" (49). In other words, resignation is the renunciation of the world for the sake of gaining the eternal. Faith, on the other hand, is the absurd whereby the eternal comes *through* the temporal.

Thus, when we renounce the world, we gain the eternal; we resign ourselves to the loss of the beloved and find peace in the resignation. This "finding peace in the resignation" is the movement into our "eternal consciousness," for we remove the world and retain the self. When we have faith, however, we paradoxically gain the world and retain the self. We do not lose the self in the world, for the self has been chosen absolutely—that is, chosen in its basis, which is God. This is the opposite of gaining the world and losing the self.

Interlude

Throughout his works, Kierkegaard speaks in terms of polarities or opposites. He speaks of the eternal and the temporal. He speaks of the world and the self. He speaks of faith and resignation. He speaks of the internal and external. Kierkegaard then relates these terms to each other in various ways and in various places. Thus, the self is able to gain the world (the temporal) through faith, but this it can do only by first choosing itself rather than the world. Further, in choosing itself it relates itself to the absolute, which is God. But if the self makes its relationship to God similar to its relationship to any other thing or object, even the beloved, God then becomes another thing in the world. Further still, the universal can apparently appear as the absolute, but the universal is true for all humans whereas the absolute is true only for the individual. God is the absolute, but love, often associated with God, either as God's love for us or our love for God, is in the realm of the universal. But we can approach God only through the individual, and the individual, when chosen as self, rises above the universal (*Fear and Trembling*, 55).

The contradictions and confusions that emerge throughout Kierkegaard's writings, like the profusion of mushrooms in a damp, shaded woods, like the abundance of thistles in an open, sun-drenched meadow, or like the plethora of dandelions in a well-watered lawn, are the result of his constantly shifting ways of relating these opposite terms to each other. But even in his self-consciousness of the contradictions inherent in his thinking, Kierkegaard continues to think in his convoluted ways, an example of which is found in the upbuilding discourse titled "To Gain One's Soul in Patience." There he says, "[i]n the eternal there is no such self-contradiction, but not because it, like the temporal, either is or is not, but because it is" (*Eighteen Upbuilding Discourses*, Kierkegaard, 1843/1990, 163). Continuing in the same vein, Kierkegaard goes on to say, "[t]hen this self-contradiction must be sought, if anywhere, in the internal, but the internal is, after all, in its most universal expression, the soul" (163). And finally he concludes, "[t]he soul is the contradiction of the temporal and the eternal, and here, therefore, the same thing can be possessed and the same thing gained and at the same time" (163).

When he talks about the soul, Kierkegaard seems to mean something other than the self, yet he uses the term in the same way as the term *self*. He says, "[h]is soul is a self-contradiction between the external and the internal, the temporal and the eternal. It is a self-contradiction, because wanting to express the contradiction within itself is precisely what makes it what it is." Therefore, "soul is in contradiction and is self-contradiction" (166). It is as if the soul is the point at which the temporal and the eternal meet, while it itself is neither. Yet, it could also be that the soul is thereby in contradiction either with itself or with the self. The soul is to be gained and possessed, but this can be only if there is a self who can gain and possess it. Thus, Kierkegaard says, "[c]onsequently he gains ... his soul from God, away from the world, through himself" (167).

Yet the soul, being in contradiction, is in a struggle, and this struggle is with the eternal, God, and the self. "[T]his struggle is such that the person who loses the eternal loses God and himself, and the person who loses God loses the eternal and himself, and the person who loses himself loses the eternal and God" (199). Clearly, then, when the self chooses itself it also chooses the eternal and God, both of which come with choosing the self. The soul seems to be the point at which these different yet identical aspects come together. The self cannot be what it is without being in God. The soul is the power to pull the self together, to keep the self from being fragmented and dispersed, and the power to pull the self out of the suffering of life so that it does not founder on the shoals of the world. It also appears to be that which relates the self to God.

The soul seems to be for Kierkegaard that which has to be gained by the self, and yet, once gained, to be the guiding power of the self. The self stands in danger in life, not the least of which is the loss of the self itself (*The Sickness unto Death*, Kierkegaard, 1849/1980, 32). It is the strength of the soul that allows the self to maintain the necessary inwardness of standing firm as a whole, not fragmented, self in the face of the dangers inherent in life and in the world. In the face of these dangers, what can a person hold onto, and what can be safeguarded for oneself? Since life is totally uncertain, what can be truly preserved, and what is worthy of preserving? Kierkegaard says, "What else could that be but a person's soul?" (*Eighteen Upbuilding Discourses*, 185).

Explication of the Religious

The soul comes from God as the power to keep the self God-centered rather than world-centered. Yet the world encroaches on the self, because the self lives in the world. The self, even though in choosing itself it chooses God, suffers from the world and its position in the world. The self is weak in itself and lives in perpetual anxiety, because in its eternal aspect the self lives in the moment (*The Concept of Anxiety*, Kierkegaard 1844/1980, 87). Being in the moment, for that moment there is no past and no future. All is indeterminate and uncertain. The self, however, desires certainty and security, so it tends to turn toward the world for this. But the world is not the self's true nature except insofar as the self begins with this single individual (for the world, i.e., Nature, creates everything as single individual things). The self's true nature is the eternal. That is, the self, by choosing itself, chooses itself in its eternal aspect, thereby choosing God also, since God is the eternal. Therefore, if the self is eternal in its nature, and if God is the eternal, then God is the self's true nature.

Yet since the self can lose itself in the world, fragmenting itself and tormenting itself in its fragmentation (*Christian Discourses*, Kierkegaard, 1848/1940), it must remain mindful of its true nature. This comes from the power of the soul, which comes from God. When the self chooses itself absolutely, it enters into an absolute relation with the absolute, God. Thus, when the self chooses itself, it also receives the empowered soul, which comes from God and which maintains the integrity of the self. In maintaining the integrity of the self, the soul helps the self to maintain its relation to itself and thereby its relation to God. So where the self, in its stance in the world, seeks to win the world for itself, to provide its security and to give it a temporal position in and as the external thing, which it relates to through the universal ethic of love, it can only "win the world" through faith. For, if the self seeks to win the world through its own desire and will for the world, then it will lose not only that which it seeks, but the self will also lose its soul—that is, itself.

The self can go on living in the world without its soul, but only through the inner movement of resignation, by which it resigns itself to having lost the world by means of having lost that which it loves in the world. The self fades away in this case, because it has no soul. But if the self can return to itself through this loss, because it regrets seeking itself in the world, then the self is restored to itself through the power of the soul, and in the faith that it has not lost itself, the world is won at last. The world does not constitute the self in this case. The self is constituted by that which it chooses, namely itself in its eternal aspect. The self stands in that which is also chosen when the self chooses itself in its eternal aspect, and this is God. Through God the soul enters the self, which is the power of the self to maintain itself in itself and in God, even while living in the world. This, then, becomes the religious self, the self who realizes that it and God stand in a unique relation to each other.

I now turn this study to an examination of what it means existentially to be a self. The self is an existential self. That is, it exists as a self. But since a self is no thing, this involves an inherent subjectivity without an object. This pure subjectivity is existentially experienced as anxious being.

Chapter 4

ANXIETY AND THE SUBJECTIVE

As we have seen, it is our choice to choose the self. At a particular point in life, we realize that the world will not suffice as the center of our life, and we are faced with the choice of either continuing to pursue the world or to choose the self. We must choose to be a self, for we cannot depend on the world to provide us with a self. The failure of the world to provide us with the conditions for our completion makes this choice unavoidable. When we choose to be a self, there is the paradoxical effect of placing the individual above the universal, and of putting the individual's relation with God above the ethical duty we have toward others.

Another paradox emerges in this mandatory choosing of the self. That is the development of anxiety as the existential experience of becoming a self. Kierkegaard introduces the concept of anxiety in a work of that same title, *The Concept of Anxiety* (Kierkegaard, 1844/1980). This concept is derived from his reflections on Adam and original sin. The original sin of Adam is based in the fact that he is, as all humans are, a synthesis of body and soul. These two aspects are united in the spirit (43).

The spirit that unites the individual in body and soul is precisely that which makes us human. It is the human spirit and at the same time the divine spirit, for we are "also a synthesis of the temporal and the eternal" (85). The spirit brings an openness to the human individual, an openness that is experienced as possibility. The possibility for the human individual is to *be*. But this possibility is the actuality of freedom (42). Thus, the spirit is the human's realization of the possibility of being, and in this realization of possibility is the actual way of being that is ours to be, namely as free being. That is, the freedom that is implicit in possibility is our human mode of being. Put another way, human being is freedom itself.

We are free beings, beings who are free to choose to be a self or not, and in this freedom lies the possibility for us to be other than we are, namely, free. That is, we have the possibility to reject our basic spiritual freedom. This freedom is the source of a fundamental and inherent anxiety. For we live in this freedom, which is indeterminate possibility. We live in the "dizziness of freedom" (61) and thus experience our life anxiously. This anxiety is different from fear, for fear always has an object that is feared. Anxiety, however, has no object because it is how we experience the way of our being in the freedom of possibility. Our existential anxiety has as its "object" a nothingness that is yet something, or conversely, a "something" that is in reality the nothingness, or not-yet-being, that real possibility is. For, possibility is indeterminate, without form, otherwise it would be actuality. Insofar as this is our mode of being, in our being as freedom, there is the anxiety of having no form. Or, rather, our "form" is spirit, but spirit has no form and thus is free spirit.

Kierkegaard says that the "human being is spirit. But what is spirit? Spirit is the self" (*The Sickness unto Death*, 13). In the human individual, the spirit is a formless possibility projecting its actuality as freedom (*The Concept of Anxiety*, 41). We have seen elsewhere that the self must be chosen absolutely—that is, freely. Thus, in its nature as freedom, the spirit as self can only choose itself. It is free to be itself. The human individual, in realizing himself as spirit, as this individual self, is choosing the self in this individual form. This choosing the self is at the same time choosing God (107). When we stand as this individual self we simultaneously stand before God. As free spirit, the only form the spirit can project itself into is to actualize itself as a self.

Yet, once we choose the self in freedom and find ourselves standing before God, we immediately realize our basic guilt because of the sin of willfulness. For, as a self who has freely chosen itself as this individual, we have acted as willing individuals, because we are free spirits. We can only choose to be a self, yet such a choice results in guilt, because we spontaneously stand before God when we stand as this individual self. In standing before the eternal, infinite, and absolute God, we can stand only as this temporal, finite, and individual self. Because we are not God, yet upon becoming a self we find ourselves before God, we realize immediately the willfulness of our choice, and we feel guilty even though it was a necessary choice. Put another way, in the perfect freedom of the spirit, it is in its very nature to project the actuality of its freedom into the form of a self. However, upon becoming a self, the self as self is imperfect. Thus, an imperfect self standing before a perfect God can only feel guilty because of its imperfection before the perfect. Thus, we are in sin because of choosing the self absolutely, and we are guilty because of being an imperfect self before God.

However, if the spirit is freedom, then it is eternal, infinite, and absolute. That is to say, it is spirit as God. But prior to its becoming a self, it does not know itself as God. Thus, if it is inherent in the spirit to become a self, then this also means that it is inherent in the spirit to realize itself as God. In this regard, Kierkegaard says that "when the finite spirit would see God, it must begin as guilty" (*The Concept of Anxiety*, 107). He goes on to say that "freedom, as soon as guilt is posited, returns as repentance" (109). Repentance, as we have seen earlier, is the turning of the self toward itself. Now we can see that in the self's turning toward itself, it is actually the spirit projecting itself as self before itself as God. Self and God, therefore, are the two aspects that necessarily emerge as the spirit moves toward the actualization of itself, an actualization that must necessarily be realized in its nature as absolute freedom. Put another way, we can see that in order for spirit to know itself as God, it must become itself as self. More specifically, self can only be as this human individual self. The immediate sense of guilt experienced by the individual is a guilt of ignorance. The individual self does not know itself as spirit, and it does not see its true relation with God.

For Kierkegaard, there are only two ways in which the truth of our existential nature is known by us. We know this truth either through a recollection, which presumes that we already have this knowledge in us and only have to be reminded of it, or through being enlightened to this knowledge from another external source (*Philosophical Fragments*, Kierkegaard 1844/1985, 9–10). But it is not only some objective knowledge about the truth of our human nature that is being considered here. Rather, it is our human individual existence, lived in the moment of existing, that we are attempting to understand. Insofar as any thing's essential nature would be difficult to fathom from a thing's existence (for, where could we possibly begin?), the same is infinitely more true about our individual existence. Our true nature, or the truth about our nature, must necessarily be given in our existence. In other words, our essence must be inherent in our existence.

In *Philosophical Fragments*, Kierkegaard says repeatedly that there is an inherent paradox in our knowledge of our essence that is derived from our existence. The paradox is that our thinking seeks to know something that it cannot think (37). This means that we cannot expect to be able to identify our essence, our nature, from the attempt to understand our existence. Thought can only think about something that appears in historical time, something, that is, that comes into being in historical time. But our existence is not such a thing that can be understood by thought, because for us as individual beings, as individual self, our existence is purely subjective. I can "know" only my own existence, but in its immediacy it is outside of historical time. Thus, my individual existence is such that it is not "known" in the same way that a tree or a rock is known.

The paradox about my existence is that I can only attempt to describe it in the same way that I describe a tree or a rock. In this attempt, I end up in falsehood, in untruth, and I might as well not have attempted in the first place. My individual existence is not a matter for thought, because it is a spiritual reality. It is my existence that is spiritual, since it is purely subjective and cannot be objectified in thought without becoming false. In the work *Concluding Unscientific Postscript to Philosophical Fragments* (Kierkegaard, 1846/1992) Kierkegaard moves directly into the subjective nature of existence with the statement: "The knowing spirit is an existing spirit, and … every human being is such a spirit existing for himself" (189).

Kierkegaard is concerned only with taking his own individual subjective existence as the true starting point for arriving at the knowledge of the truth about his own individual subjective existence. He is engaged in a paradoxical activity, for he is attempting to arrive at some kind of objective statement about his existence from standing directly within his existence.

He *is* his existence. The fact that he can say objectively that his existence is a spiritual existence rests in the fact that he *is* his existence. He exists, and he knows it subjectively. He is not saying that he is a self or soul who comes into being and then becomes aware of being, as Kierkegaard's predecessor Hegel implied. Kierkegaard is saying that because he is subjectively aware of existing, and because the subjective experience of existing and the awareness of it occur in one and the same moment, that therefore his existence can only be spiritual. For, there is no *thing* that exists. The subjective experience of existing is not that his body exists. His body is one object among many in the world. The subjective experience of existing is inwardly known. This is the spirit, though not objectively postulated as an objective "something" that comes into oneself from somewhere. Taking the subjective experience of existing as the only real starting point for discovering and knowing the truth about our existence, the only reality that we can know directly because we stand in existence, Kierkegaard realizes that what is known thereby is his paradoxical relation to the true. It is in this subjective relation to the true (existence) as we know it (subjectively) that we see the reality of the spiritual. For, the spirit's reality is the self's relating to the true, the immediately present relating to the eternally present, which is God (199). Kierkegaard adds a telling comment in a footnote on the next page: "In this way God is not a postulate, but the existing person's postulating of God is—a necessity" (200).

It remains to understand how it is that the existing person, who in truth exists subjectively—that is, whose existence and subjectivity are one and the same moment—finds it to be a necessity that God be postulated. When we turn our thought to discovering the true, not only true for now but in an absolute sense the *truth*, we are necessarily seeking something eternal. Yet, because we take as our starting point the subjective experience of existing, we immediately see that *this* individual's existence, *my* existing, is true. I cannot deny that I am existing, though I can certainly doubt it, as did Descartes. But to doubt what I subjectively *know* as true, namely that I am, I exist, is to engage in mere speculative thinking. As soon as I begin to think speculatively, I am seeking objective truth. I erroneously believe that only objective truth can establish the certitude of universal truth—that is, true for all people and for all time. Thus, to say that God exists is to speak a universal and objective "truth." But this is actually an untruth, because the starting point for this statement assumes the existence of something else, namely the knowing subject, which is, of course, the only reality that *I* can know immediately and directly. For, I am that subjective immediate experience of existing, and therefore I am the subjective knower. This experience is the anxiety of existing, which is the anxiety of freedom, and thus I seek something objective, some objective truth, to limit my freedom and to alleviate my anxiety.

This desire, however, can lead to an erroneous objectification. If I say, for example, that since I exist I must have been created and that, therefore, God exists as my creator, I fall into error. For, this statement fails to take into account the fact that my subjective experience of existing has no temporal point of coming into existence. *I* was not created in the same sense as my body was. The subjective experience of existing is immediate, and the absolutely immediate has no past or future. Therefore, I, the self, was not created in any sense of the term.

However, on the two grounds of, first, that I am seeking the truth about my existence, and, second, that my subjective experience of existing is atemporal—that is, outside of time—I come to the resolution that God also is atemporal. I postulate this, because in my subjective experience of existing, in the freedom and anxiety of it, the truth that I seek about it is that I exist in an eternal way. That is, my self is chosen in its eternal aspect, the freedom of spirit. Even though I live my life as this individual, the actual experience of existing is not the same as living life. In living my life as an individual, I live from morning to night, from one activity to the next. I live my life—that is, temporally and finitely. However, with each moment that I am subjectively aware of existing, I enter a relation with the eternal. For that timeless moment, my living of life is put into suspension as I stand in relation to the eternal, the "outside of time." Kierkegaard points this out clearly. The "eternal truth [subjectively existing] has come into existence in time [the individual who lives life]" (*Concluding Unscientific Postscript*, 209). For that timeless moment, I stand in relation to my eternal aspect. That is, I stand in relation to God, and God stands in relation to me. Since both self and God arise in the same subjective experience of existing, my subjective experience of existing (the atemporal) stands in relation to the historical fact of my existence (the temporal). The subjective experience is the self in its eternal aspect. God is the name of this eternal aspect of existing, not existence itself.

Speculative philosophy posits the objective category of existence, or being, as the objective reality of God, both as substance (essence) and as cause. Thus, objectively speaking, in the manner of Spinoza, God's essence *is* his existence. Therefore, God *is*. This approach, however, begins with the presumption of preexisting abstract categories of reality, such as "essence," "cause," "substance," etc. Kierkegaard, rather, begins with the only directly experienced reality, that of the subjective experience of the existing individual. In this experience, the existing subject stands in direct relation to his existence. The self stands in relation to itself but in the form of the finite standing in relation to the infinite, or in the form of the temporal standing in relation to the eternal. Since both pairs of opposites inhere in the subjective experience of existing itself, and since it is the self who stands in relation to itself in the experience of existing, Kierkegaard says that this is the same as the temporal and finite self relating to itself in its eternal and infinite aspect. This eternal and infinite aspect of the self is God.

Inherent in this relation that emerges between self and God, which is between the self and itself in its eternal aspect, there is a distance that opens up. As the self stands before itself, before God, in this relation, there is anxiety because of the freedom and potentiality the self sees across the distance as it stands before God. It is the attempt to close this distance, to bridge the gap, that is our next consideration.

Chapter 5

THE LEAP OF FAITH

The opening sentence of *Fear and Trembling* reads like a response to Schopenhauer's great work, *The World as Will and Representation*, though according to Lowrie (1970, 488), Kierkegaard did not read Schopenhauer until the year before his death. The whole sentence is worth quoting.

> If a human being did not have an eternal consciousness, if underlying everything there were only a wild, fermenting power that writhing in dark passions produced everything, be it significant or insignificant, if a vast, never appeased emptiness hid beneath everything, what would life be then but despair? (*Fear and Trembling*, 15)

In *The Sickness unto Death*, Kierkegaard elaborates on the despair to which we humans are subject.

> If a human self had itself established itself, then there could be only one form [of despair]: not to will to be oneself, to will to do away with oneself, but

there would not be the form: in despair to will to be oneself. (14)

The self in *The Sickness unto Death* is a "synthesis of the infinite and the finite, of the temporal and the eternal, of freedom and necessity" (13). Despair comes from "the relation in which the synthesis relates itself to itself" (16). Kierkegaard explains this synthesis that relates itself to itself as the relation that a self enters when it becomes aware of being a self. The self who becomes aware of being a self enters a relation with itself by virtue of becoming aware of being a self. This relation itself is the relation that relates the two aspects of self to each other. Thus, the relation of the infinite and the finite, the temporal and the eternal, and freedom and necessity is itself the self but only when the self is related to itself—that is, when it has become aware of being a self.

This relation is the self, because it is spirit. Spirit is the relation of the opposites to each other, the synthesis of the two. In this relation, in the relation of the two, the two stand in relation to each other in the act of relating, and further, this relating is what "relates (the self) to itself and in relating itself to itself relates itself to another" (13–14). Kierkegaard points out that "[s]uch a relation that relates itself to itself, a self, must either have established itself or have been established by another" (13). Because we have not established ourselves, because we are not our own authors, there is the possibility of the second form of despair, in despair to will to be oneself.

Despair is similar to the anxiety of the dizziness of freedom, except where anxiety concerns the mode of being that the spirit is, namely freedom, despair is related to the self's willingness to either be itself or to not be itself. Lowrie (1970, 76) described Kierkegaard's concept of the relation of anxiety to despair as that, where anxiety is the individual's state of being in original sin because of being a free spirit, despair is the individual's awareness of being in sin before God. Despair, then, is equally as unavoidable for the self as anxiety is unavoidable for the spirit.

Since the spirit is the self, despair and anxiety are the two fundamental experiences of existing as a self. Anxiety is existing itself while despair is existing before that which is our author, namely God. That is, we exist as self only when we stand before God. The anxiety of existing is experienced by the self as guilt. We can only experience ourselves as guilty, hence as anxious, because of the original sin inherent in existing, which is the freedom of spirit. It is sin because of its struggle that is the attempt to be free from its source, a struggle that it cannot but be engaged in, because the spirit is freedom itself. In freedom it posits itself as a self, thereby establishing itself apart from its source, which is God.

In this anxiety, this guilt, the individual is faced with himself. Guilt, anxiety, withdraws the awareness of the self away from its pursuit of itself in and through the world and inward toward itself. The self, in turning inward, finds itself guilty, and this brings about repentance (*The Concept of Anxiety*, 107). Repentance is the focus of the self upon itself in such a way that it must choose itself as a self. The self creates itself in choosing to be responsible for itself. In other words, the self takes responsibility for the sin of the spirit, which in its own nature is freedom itself. The self is chosen by itself, and freely chosen, because the spirit is itself freedom. Thus, from our freedom comes our original sin, because in choosing to be a self the self separates itself from God.

We have seen how God is necessarily posited by the self as the author and source of the self. Therefore, when the self chooses itself, it simultaneously chooses God. In positing itself, the self posits God. In positing itself and God, the self brings itself into a relation with God. Self is posited as finite and God as infinite. Thus, in choosing to be a self, the self establishes itself as a finite expression of the infinite, as a temporal manifestation of the eternal, and as an individual expression of the universal or absolute. This is what Kierkegaard meant when he spoke of the self choosing itself absolutely and thereby entering into an absolute relation with the absolute (*Fear and Trembling*, 56).

The self stands as a self before God, the source of self, since God is the infinite and eternal power that first established the relation that the self is. The self, however, stands in sin and stands in the anxiety of guilt before God. This brings upon the self the experience of despair. The self despairs before God, because it either wills to not be a self, or it wills to be a self. These two forms of despair are both rooted in the self's guilt (anxiety) for its sin (in freedom to be a self) before God. The self does not realize, however, that God is the self in its eternal aspect (*The Sickness unto Death*, 79). The self's reaction is the first form of despair, "in despair to will to be rid of [it]self" (20). If the self could cease to be a self, its sin and guilt would also cease. If the self ceased to be, then also God would cease to be, and there would no longer be the constituents of the self's sin and guilt.

But this willing to cease to be a self is itself despair, because such a willing is futile. For, to will to cease to be a self implies the possibility of reversing the original choice to be a self. But possibility is freedom, and freedom is spirit. It is the nature of spirit to freely establish itself as freedom; that is, as what it is, namely a self. Thus, to will to cease to be a self is an impossibility because of the inherent contradiction in such a willing. The spirit cannot go against itself, or rather, it cannot succeed in willing to go against itself. Thus, to will this is to will it in despair.

The second form of this despair is to will to be oneself. This willing is the willing to remove God from the relation. The self would be itself alone, and therefore if God is removed then there is no other before whom the self would be guilty. But this is an impossibility, because it contradicts the original choice to be a self, which simultaneously brings God into the relation. The self cannot be free of God, because God cannot be removed from the relation, since God is the very relation of the self's relating itself to itself.

In this convoluted manner of speaking, Kierkegaard is pointing out that when the self chooses to be itself, it simultaneously establishes itself in God. But this establishment is such that there is a concomitant separation of self from God since there is a relation between the two. This sense of separation is our human sin, experienced as the anxiety of existing as an individual self. In Kierkegaard's words, "[s]in is: before God in despair not to will to be oneself, or before God in despair to will to be oneself" (*The Sickness unto Death*, 81). The guilt of this sin is absolute, because we stand in an absolute relation to the absolute. We stand intrinsically guilty before God because of our separation from God. We despair of ourselves in guilt and seek to be rid of our absolute guilt by willing to either not be a self or by willing to be a self but not before God. Either way, our willing is bound to be futile, hence we end in despair.

A Summary of Our Existential Situation

Our whole life is involved with attempting to deal with our existential anxiety. We live as individuals. This is what we are by birth. As individuals, we live with an awareness of being separated, cut off, and isolated from the whole. The idea of the whole is initially the whole world, as pointed out in *Either/Or*. But we cannot return to the world as our wholeness because of the reasons pointed out earlier. So when we choose to be what we are; that is, when we willingly choose to be individuals, we also choose to be a self. Our existential anxiety, then, takes on the quality of guilt. We inwardly interpret this guilt as sinfulness, because in our existence as a self we find ourselves in a relation with the absolute. It is because of the absoluteness of being a self that we find ourselves standing in a relation to the absolute. It is the absoluteness of this relating, and the absoluteness of the aspects of self that are in relation to each other, that causes our existential guilt to be interpreted as our inherent sinfulness. Guilt becomes sinfulness when we stand before the absolute. The absolute self is the absolute God. That is, the self in its eternal aspect can only be God. God is the self in its eternal aspect. Thus it is that the self comes to find itself standing before God, and standing before God is the existential experience of standing separated from God. This separation from God is our existential experience of sin, and thus of guilt.

In order to quell our anxiety, in order to vanquish our guilt, and in order to expiate our sinfulness, we must find a way to overcome our existential sense of separation and isolation from God. There are two ways in which we attempt to heal this split, and these two ways correspond to the two forms of despair that have been described.

The first way is the way of the mystic. This corresponds to the will to cease to be as a self. The mystic seeks to negate the sense of self by returning to a mergence with the absolute, God, which is to return to a primordial state prior to the creation of a self, thus, prior to the separation of self from God. The mystic sees the situation as being that the self is the aspect of human existence that separates the individual from realizing its essential oneness with God. Thus, if we negate the self we will simultaneously rejoin with God in mystical oneness. Yet, if God is the self in its absolute and eternal aspects, might we end up in the situation in which to eradicate one is to eradicate the other? This is suggested by considering that throughout the whole history of mysticism, mystics have posited the essentially transcendent God, the God who is both All and Nothing, "which no language but that of negation can define" (Underhill 1911, 344–45).

The language of mysticism is as varied as are its cultural traditions. This quest for the submersion of the self into God is expressed as the "marriage between God and the soul" (quoted in Underhill, 1911, 343). The mystic seeks the True Self, the Divine Abyss, the true Country of the Soul, all of which phrases refer to the same reality that one enters upon dissolving the self in the Godhead. However it is described, Kierkegaard sees the mystical as a form of spiritual aestheticism (Collins 1953), as well as the individual's absolute choosing of himself (*Either/Or*, 245).Though mystics often speak of choosing God, he says, "yet substantially ... this comes to the same thing" (246). In the end, the self disappears into God, which would be equivalent to the self imploding upon itself.

The second way of resolving the existential anxiety inherent in our existence, the way corresponding to the second form of despair, the will to be as a self, is to strive to fully be a self. This is the way of the stoic. The stoic accepts his life as a self-responsible moral agent regardless of what happens in that life. James (1902) quotes Marcus Aurelius as saying, "[i]t is a man's duty to comfort himself and wait for the natural dissolution" (42). The stoic takes hold of the self and is a self in full possession of itself. Kierkegaard sees this as a form of spiritual ethics whereby an individual creates for himself personal virtues that enable him to live as fully a self as he can on his own. These are virtues, such as courage, temperance, valor, and moderation, which resemble religious virtues but are in actuality more Greek, which is to say, stoic (*Either/Or*, 245). In other words, the self stands alone in the world, depending upon himself alone, self-determined by adherence to the universal ruling reason. In effect, God has disappeared into the world order, becoming identified as the universal ruling reason. The God before whom the self stands is gone.

Toward the Leap of Faith

Both of these quasi-religious forms of dealing with our existential anxiety, guilt, and sinfulness before God do not maintain the self in the truthfulness of itself. The truth of the self is always, according to Kierkegaard, "that directly before which it is a self" (*The Sickness unto Death*, 79). At this point, Kierkegaard distinguishes between the human self, on the one hand, that is first ignorant of being an eternal self, such as is the case with the stoics, then, becoming aware of having an eternal aspect, is preoccupied with this to the detriment of the self. This results in the mystic's determination to be only the eternal in a mergence with God, or in the stoic's determination to be a self alone without God. On the other hand, there is what Kierkegaard calls the "theological self," which is "the self directly before God" (79). This self is conscious of existing before God and is the transformed human self whose criterion is God. Thus, the self finally realizes that its criterion—that is, that which makes it what it is, namely God—is that directly before which it is a self. This means that the self realizes that it is a self only when it stands before God. This is the theological self, which is distinguished from the human self who is not aware of this criterion.

Kierkegaard says that "[n]ot until a self as this specific single individual is conscious of existing before God, not until then is it the infinite self" (80). When we are fully conscious that we are a self only when we stand before God—that is, when we are conscious that being a self means being an infinite self—then we realize that our self and God are the two aspects of our individual existence that has become aware of itself, and that this awareness stands in an absolute relation with itself. We no longer live in a world without God, nor are we without God in the world. We have come to be fully and willingly a self before God, and this is to be transparently in God. This is the transition from despair to faith. "Faith is: that the self in being itself and in willing to be itself rests transparently in God" (82). Despair ends when the self "in relating itself to itself and in willing to be itself … rests transparently in the power that established it" (14). The power that established the self is the self's criterion, God.

To rest transparently in God is to willingly exist before God as we are. Before God we are guilty because of being in sin. Kierkegaard puts it this way: "What really makes human guilt into sin is that the guilty one has the consciousness of existing before God" (80). The original form our sin takes, as we have seen earlier, is inherent in the form of existence that we as humans live, namely to be as a self. For, in being a self, we are separated from our source. Now, we have seen Kierkegaard define sin as either of the two forms of despair. It is the despair that is the "sickness unto death" and it is in sin that we will to either remove the self or remove God from the relation in which both are established. Sin is to maintain this separation and to attempt to resolve it by removing one or the other of the aspects of our individual existence. Further, as long as we attempt to do this, we are in despair.

The more we attempt to willingly not be a self before God or to be a self without God, the more we despair; and the more we despair the greater is the chance of truly losing the self. This "greatest hazard of all, losing the self" (32), comes about when we deny either constituent of our existence. The self cannot live in the abstractness of either infinity or isolation. To exist and to know that one exists before God is what distinguishes the human from all other animals. To know this existentially is the single experience that could make us "instantly go mad or sink into nothingness" (32). It is simply too great a realization for us to handle in our normal ways of dealing with life's other contradictions and paradoxes. We cannot resolve this by reducing one term to another or by positing either as prior to the other. For, where being a self is concerned, being a self before God is present as well. Where being a self before God is the realization, being a self before God in sin is realized as well. In short, there is no way to be a self without being a self before God, and there is no way to be a self before God without being a self before God in sin.

Spiritually, such a state of existence results in only one effect. We despair, and despair is the spiritual sickness that assails us, for we want to hide our faces in shame, which is a subtle way to remove God, or we want to endlessly flagellate ourselves into the submissiveness of self-negation as perpetual penance. We cannot lift ourselves out of despair in either of these two ways.

The only way out of despair is through faith. But faith is not despair's opposite. Faith is despair's transformation, for both are the result of being a self before God in sin. Where despair is the realization of the distance between self and God, the distance that is the sin of separation and being cut off from our source, faith is the realization that sin actually connects us to God, but only if we stand transparently in our sin and not try to hide it or to negate it. It is the willingness to be transparent before God as a self that is the mark of faith. Faith is, then, the trust that if we stand before God acknowledging that we are in sin because we are a self, that our sin will be "forgiven" and our relation with God restored. Our sin is "forgiven" because rather than being the wedge that drives self and God further apart, rather than slipping more and more into separation out of despair, our sin itself—that is, our separation as a self—becomes the connective link that restores our relation with God, but only if we stand transparently in it as the self that we are. Being transparent is to have no content, no criterion, other than God, who is posited along with the positing of the self. We may be a husband, a wife, a father, a mother, a banker, teacher, or nurse, but this is not who we are; this is not our content. Our content, our criterion, is the synthesis of the finite and the infinite, the temporal and the eternal, the synthesis of self *and* God, not self *or* God. The realization of this is to be transparently before God. This is the leap of faith.

It remains now to examine how Kierkegaard understands the position of Christianity in the development of faith, forgiveness, and the reconciliation of self to God. This will lead us to the fundamental question that separates Judaism from Christianity, which is, do we need a mediator to give us forgiveness of our basic sin, or is this a responsibility that each individual has alone, to stand alone before God in sin and in the forgiveness of sin?

Chapter 6

TO BE CHRISTIAN

Up to now the primary focus has been on the individual self's relation to God. This has not been a categorical relationship—that is, a relationship between categorical entities with self on one side and God on the other. It has not been a discussion about conceptualizing this relation as being between a thinking, feeling, desiring, and fearing subject on the one hand, and a judging, willing God as object on the other. God is not an objective "thing," however supreme and absolute. God is, rather, the existential infinite and eternal aspect of the existential finite and temporal self. God and self arise together in the existential experience of being an existing self.

God does not "forgive" the sin of being a self. Sin, as we have seen, is in the separation between self and God that is opened up by the choice we make to be a self. The "forgiveness" of this sin comes in the qualitative change in the relation between self and God, such that the separation is no longer experienced as the abyss of nothingness, as pointed out in *The Sickness unto Death* (122), that we despair of ever crossing or bridging. In the qualitative change, the separation becomes the opportunity for a new way for the self to stand before God.

For Kierkegaard this consideration leads directly to Christianity, or, more specifically, to Christ as the prototype "Christian." Before continuing the discussion, two points need to be cleared up concerning the existential inconsistency of Kierkegaard's thinking in this context. He seems to leave the existential and enter the dogmatic when he begins to look at the person of Jesus Christ. In the first place, when Kierkegaard examines the life of Christ, he speaks of it as exemplary of a voluntary self-denial and suffering for the sake of God, or for the sake of the doctrine that Christ puts forth to his disciples (*Judge for Yourself*, Kierkegaard, 1851/1990, 205). It may be thought that Kierkegaard presents Christ as doing exactly what constitutes one form of despair, namely to will to cease to be as a self. Christ actually accomplishes this in the extreme as he willingly goes to his death on the cross. Along the same line, when Christ calls out, "My God, why have you forsaken me?", the scene demonstrates that when we surrender the self in the negation of voluntary death, real or symbolic, we may also find ourselves feeling even more separated from God. However, we shall see that Christ's self-denial on the cross has a more existentially relevant interpretation.

The second point in which Kierkegaard seems to enter contradiction is when he presents Christianity as a system in one work, *The Sickness unto Death*, while stating that this absolutely cannot be the method for presenting Christ's teachings (*Attack upon Christianity*, Kierkegaard, 1855/1944, 40). What Kierkegaard does in this systemization is to objectify both the self and God. He objectifies the self by saying that we must imitate Christ, and he objectifies God by saying that in following Christ we look upon him as our redeemer in his role as the God-man (*The Sickness unto Death*, 118).

Our concern here is not with Kierkegaard as the Christian apologist, but with Kierkegaard as the existential Christian theologian. But our concern is also to not be presented with any system of dogmatic theology or system of beliefs that would lead to objectifying what begins in the existential moment of choosing to be a self. For, to objectify God, or to posit a set of dogma that would be open to doubt, or to present us with the doctrine of looking to another for the forgiveness of sin and for the salvation of our soul, is to leave the existential and to enter theology by way of dogmatic and traditional doctrine.

For the purpose of this study, we shall stay with the existential Kierkegaard and examine how Christianity represents the qualitative change in the relation of self and God when we stand in existential transparency before God. What is there in Christianity and in Christ's teachings that exemplifies for us what this qualitative change is that comes with the leap of faith? It must be something that develops within the individual self as it stands transparently before God. It must be some quality that traverses the abyss between self and God, and that emerges as the only power that can do so. It must also be something that is possible to be experienced existentially— that is, experienced within the existing individual self as the self faces not only God but the world as well. In other words, as the self stands before God, yet facing God across a chasm, an abyss, there must be something that goes out from one to the other that links them both across the abyss. It is faith, according to Kierkegaard, that lays the ground for this, for faith is the acknowledgment that it is possible to bridge the separation between self and God, a separation that is the very nature of the relation between self and God.

To look at the dynamics of faith more closely, when we first choose to be a self, we also bring God into an existential relation with us. Or, conversely, we bring ourselves into an existential relation with God. When we choose to be a self, we at the same time create a relation between the self and

God. The relation is possible only in separation, for where there is a relation, there is also an implicit separation. For relation consists of two parts standing before each other, or, as Kierkegaard says, the relation is the third or synthesis of the two (*The Sickness unto Death*, 13).

As soon as we become existentially aware of being a self—that is, as soon as we choose to be a self—we become aware of the self as standing before God, which is the self's eternal aspect. Thus, it is inevitable that God first appears to us as Other. We are ignorant at first of God's being the self in its eternal aspect, and we see God as the absolute Other. That is, when we choose to be a self, we look out from our finite self and see in the distance, across a vast chasm or abyss, God as the absolute Other, because God is the infinite. The chasm is actually, of course, within our own consciousness, but while we remain ignorant of the true nature of the self's eternal aspect, God seems to be totally Other and unreachable. Yet, precisely because God emanates from the nature of the self in its eternal aspect and appears across a chasm, we develop an immediate longing to cross the abyss and join God.

Such a longing can leave us feeling even more isolated and cut off, and in despair. But when we recall how we love another person, believing that he or she will be the source of our self's completion in the world, we see that it is the act of loving that makes this belief seem true. Thus also is our love involved when we stand facing across an abyss that which will truly complete us, precisely because that Other, God, *is* the self in its eternal aspect. We learn that it is love, and love alone, that has the power to span that abyss that has self on one side and God on the other. Now, because we have chosen the self absolutely, and this choice has brought us into an absolute relation with the absolute, we realize that the love we need to have for God is absolute love (*Fear and Trembling*, 73). In the human world, when we love another, the other may or may not love us back. Whether or not our beloved loves us in return, we continue to love him or her, although we may eventually find that our act of loving wanes if the beloved continues to be unresponsive. With God, however, our love must be absolute in the sense that it is impossible for it to wane because of there being no response from the beloved. With God as our beloved, as the *only* Other who can complete us, there is no question of not being loved in return. As the eternal aspect of the self, God's "response" is inherent in our reaching across the abyss with love born of the longing we feel when we first see God "out there."

Thus, there is another dimension involved in loving God that is not present in human love. It is that in loving God we are actually loving ourselves, since God is the self in its eternal aspect. Since loving ourselves is involved in loving God, we begin to feel that God loves us in return. In other words, when we love any other, especially God, we really love what Kierkegaard calls "the *other* I" (*Works of Love*, Kierkegaard 1847/1995, 57). But in human love, this "other I" is more imaginary than real, whereas in loving God as the "other I," it is more real since God *is* the self in its eternal aspect. This is, then, really self-love, and it is a prerequisite for truly loving God. Only when self-love is present in the love for God do we feel, and are we assured, that God loves us in return. Again, Kierkegaard says, "To love God is to love oneself truly" (107). This is similar to the repentance that turns us toward the self, because we choose to be a self transparently before God. Loving God is to willingly be a self before God, and when we are existentially transparent before God, we are totally open to God. The result is that we feel that God loves us in return. This feeling of being loved by God results because in being existentially transparent before God, the willingness to be so is faith, and from faith comes love as the bridging of the chasm between self and God. When the chasm is bridged, sin is eradicated, since sin is the separation between self and God. With sin being eradicated because the separation is bridged, we feel forgiven. Thus, since it is love that bridges the chasm, it is love that "forgives."

Kierkegaard implies that with Christianity this doctrine of love first came upon the human scene. For the Jews of the Old Testament, the human relation to God was one of obedience and fear, with forgiveness of sins being brought about through sacrifice. Indeed, in *Fear and Trembling* Kierkegaard covers this theme of God testing Abraham's allegiance by demanding a sacrifice. This is not, however, an existential situation based on the self-God relation. With the arrival of Christ, on the other hand, God, the eternal aspect of the self, is brought into immediate proximity to the self. This new relation can be based only in love, and for one moment in history it was personified by one who understood the true relation of self and God. The single most important message that Jesus tried to convey to those who would listen to him was that love is the only power that can forgive sins. This is because love, much more effectively than obedience and fear, is the real power that relates the self and God across the abyss. It is the only existential way to bridge the chasm between self and God, for it is based on, rooted in, and derived from the existential dynamics that follow upon the initial choice to be a self. The Christian doctrine that Christ is the way is not to be understood as having to believe in Christ as the way to salvation. The proper understanding, according to Kierkegaard, is that Christ is the example of a human individual who realized that love heals the sin of separation and that God can be truly approached and brought closer through love (*Works of Love*, 281–82).

Of course, in the Old Testament, the Israelites are often told to love the Lord God with all their hearts (for example,

Deut. 6:5). But since this was not specifically for forgiveness of their sins, it did not really bridge the chasm between them and God. Jesus, however, offered the Israelites, who were after all Jesus's own people, a new way of understanding this "love for God" teaching of their prophets. Jesus became the "prototype" of this new way of relating the self to God (*Judge for Yourself*, 188–89). This is because he taught the forgiveness of sins through God's love, and he expressed God's love everywhere he went. Jesus was the first who totally forgot himself in his love for God (*Works of Love*, 281). In this way he forgot the self side of the relation and became the God side in full measure. It was in this way that Jesus was Christ and could legitimately go about preaching God's love and forgiving sins in the name of God's love.

For Kierkegaard this is the true meaning of Christianity, to follow Christ as the example of the proper way of relating the self to God. Real or true Christianity does not lie in accepting this or that doctrinal dogma, for that is what has made Christianity into what Kierkegaard calls "Christendom." Christendom is the legitimization, the doctrinalization, of what Christ meant. Christendom has trivialized true Christianity, which is and always has been to realize in the manner of Christ that our sins are forgiven through the love for God, and in return the love *from* God. Christendom has made this, through its plethora of Sunday sermons, into the dogma that only by believing in Christ are we saved. This is the basis of Kierkegaard's later *Attack on Christendom* (Kierkegaard 1855/1944). Christendom is a return, in Kierkegaard's mind, to the Old Testament's dependence on the "scribes and Pharisees" defining of "the Law" of the proper way to believe (120). For Kierkegaard, to believe in Christ as the savior and redeemer, while this is put forth in his more doctrinal *Christian Discourses* (Kierkegaard 1848/1940), is not as existentially true as when he speaks in a strictly existential way that the true meaning of Christianity is to be in an authentic way an authentic imitator of Christ. This is nothing more or less than to love all people as oneself, and to, through this love, forgive all of their wrongdoings toward oneself. Loving others is first based in loving God. Loving God is in turn first grounded in loving self.

This is not a doctrine to be followed dogmatically, because to do so would put all of what Christ meant into the categories of the universal ethical and of belief. As the ethical, such teachings would be impossible to be practiced, because as the ethical they fall under duty. Duty cannot love or forgive. Duty follows social morality only (*Fear and Trembling*, 55). As a set of beliefs, they are always open to doubt and persuasion. Beliefs, even the highest and most sublime, can never be existential, because the existential is absolute and therefore outside the reach of doubt and persuasion.

The truths that Christ taught derive directly from the existential self choosing itself before God. The love for God that alone can bridge the existential chasm between self and God is the result of the leap of faith by which we willingly stand before God in transparency. It is, then, through faith and love that our existential sin of separation is eradicated in being forgiven. This is the center of Christ's teachings, and of Christ himself, to love God in the faith that our sins are thereby forgiven through God's love being returned. This is to be extended to our treatment and interactions with others as we practice love, faith, and forgiveness in all our relationships. Christ was the first to do this in total self-forgetfulness, and he simply urged us to be like him. He is the way, but as an example, not as a substitute for our own existential responsibility, and not as a mediator between the individual self and God. For, this is something that we must do for ourselves, to heal our sin by bridging the chasm between self and God through faith (willingness to stand before God), and to love God, thereby experiencing God's love for us. Through this mutual love, we feel our separation (sin) being dissolved (forgiven). This is the message of Christ and the true meaning of Christianity. To practice this is truly to imitate Christ.

Chapter 7

THE THEOLOGICAL SELF

Though love for God is the ultimate way to spiritually bridge the chasm between the self and God, it is not something that can be willed. We cannot simply love God at will, even though it is the commandment of both Judaism and Christianity to love God above all else. Kierkegaard points out that it is easier to love one's neighbor than it is to love God. This is because the injunction is to love one's neighbor as oneself; whereas, the love we love God with is a self-love that becomes a self-denying love (*Works of Love*, 57–58). Erotic love is easier because in erotic love we love the beloved as our other self. But to love God is self-denying.

Kierkegaard is first and foremost an existentialist. All truth derives from the initial truth of being a self and to be a self before God. We have seen repeatedly that to be a self before God is to be in sin before God. Sin is, therefore, inevitable for Kierkegaard because it is inherent in being a self before God. Since this sin is due to being a self, it is in the existential position of being separated, cut off, and isolated from God that sin appears. God is the eternal aspect of the self, therefore being separated from God is to be separated from that which completes us. Thus, separation from God is to be an incomplete self. We can be complete only when we are able to join once again with our source of completion, the eternal aspect, God.

Standing before God as a self in sin, aware of our sinfulness because we are aware of being an individual self separated from God, results in guilt. Guilt is the feeling of responsibility for the suffering we feel in our separateness from God. Our guilt can lead us in two opposite directions. We may despair of ever being able to bridge the chasm, or we may develop faith. If we despair, we will try to get rid of the chasm by annulling one side or the other, either self or God. If we will to annul the self, we attempt to take away that self who stands before God. But in this case, God also disappears in the existential sense, even though God may remain as a theological concept. In despair, we may alternatively attempt to remove God from the relation by claiming total independence from God. The self in this case is left forever incomplete.

However, if from guilt we develop faith, then this becomes a way of standing as a self before God transparently in our sin. Since the sin is separation between the self and God, to stand before God transparently in sin is to enter the chasm with faith that it won't annihilate us in the abyss of nothingness. The only way to existentially do this is through realizing fully the self's spiritual responsibility for its relation with God and to take upon ourselves the existential effect of this. To take full responsibility for this rupture in an existentially spiritual way is to repent and humble ourselves before God, for we are the finite standing before the infinite. Repentance and humility is not something that we force ourselves to do, for in this existential moment it is a spontaneous effect of the self, in its finiteness, standing before God, in the infinity of God. If we do not take full responsibility, since we are, after all, the self who chose to be a self (albeit, necessarily as the actualization of the spirit's potential that is freedom), we will not develop faith but rather remain in a state of propitiation. Propitiation is to stand separated from God in a perpetual repentance, trying to bridge the chasm through feeling remorseful.

But this is not Kierkegaard's meaning at all. It is not God's responsibility to forgive. It is, rather, our responsibility to stand before God and, in full acknowledgement of our sin, to repent and humble ourselves before God, thereby entering the chasm through faith. This is to stand as a self in its finite aspect before the self in its infinite aspect, which is God.

Thus it is that we can bridge the chasm between the self and God only with ourselves. Since the self *is* the separation in the strict existential sense, the chasm can be bridged only by the self entering the chasm, which is to say, by the self willingly forgetting itself in self-denial. Self-denial is not the same as willing to not be a self. We have seen the Christian example of self-denial in Christ. Here Kierkegaard makes a distinction between human self-denial and Christian self-denial. "Merely human self-denial," he says, "is without fear for oneself and without regard for oneself to venture into danger" (*Works of Love*, 196). Christian self-denial, on the other hand, "makes its way to God and has its only abode in God ... [in] the very assurance that ... it is a genuine relationship to God" (195). The self, so to speak, enters self-denial by entering the chasm in faith that it enters thereby a genuine relationship with God. Since the self *is* the chasm, because only when it chooses itself does the separation open up between itself and God, by entering the chasm, the self in essence enters its own nothingness.

Kierkegaard speaks of this nothingness in the sense of the existential anxiety of being a self in *The Concept of Anxiety*. It is there that he suggests that there is a nothingness inherent in the self's desire to actualize itself (41). It is this sense of nothingness that derives from a fantasized "something," a something that is something only in fantasy, therefore in truth a nothing. For Kierkegaard this "something that is nothing" (43) appears to be the self. He says, "[d]reamily the spirit projects its own actuality, but this actuality is nothing" (41). In a later work he begins with the statement that "[a] human being is spirit. But what is spirit? Spirit is the self" (*The Sickness unto Death*, 13). These two statements together imply that in some fundamental way the self is itself the nothingness that opens up between itself and God. Thus, it seems that the spirit fantasizes itself as a self, and the conviction grows into a belief in the reality of the self when all along it is really nothing.

This idea is supported by the means of the reconciliation between self and God that Kierkegaard posits as the essence of Christ's teachings and of true Christianity. This, of course, is love, and it is indeed the single most imperative demand of Christianity. But the kind of love that Christ teaches is not at all similar to erotic love or even the love of friendship. For, these kinds of love are actually based in loving the other as the "other self" (*Works of Love*, 53). Christian love, however, is self-forgetting. It is to truly forget one's own suffering, loss, and advantages when, out of love, one puts another's suffering, loss, and advantage above one's own (281). Yet, as we have seen elsewhere, "to love God is to love oneself truly" (107). Conversely, says Kierkegaard, "to love yourself is to love God" (127). As for loving others, he says that if we love God we then love others (107), and this is the primary teaching of Christ. Kierkegaard points this out by quoting from the Gospel of John in which Christ indeed places love foremost as the way to salvation (375). Throughout this gospel, love is the major theme, and it is said that when we love others we are in truth loving God, and in loving God above ourselves we will naturally love others.

Love is self-denying and self-forgetting. The way in which we come to this is to stand transparently before God—that is, to stand before God in humility. For, to stand before God transparently is to be in the relationship of conscience with God (*The Sickness unto Death*, 124). Conscience is to acknowledge responsibility. When we acknowledge our responsibility for sin, then we are naturally humble. Thus, we can say that the way to self-denial and self-forgetfulness lies through humility before God. To stand humble before God, we stand in self-surrender. Our self no longer counts. When the self no longer counts, then the self turns toward God. We can only turn toward God out of love. Any other way of turning toward God is full of self-concern. Any other way of turning toward God would be out of fear, supplication, pleading, etc. All of this is to turn toward God for self-survival. The self still counts for something in this case, and God is a mere means to the end of self-survival, whether in this world or the next.

To turn toward God out of love, however, is to have reached the point at which the self no longer counts. To be transparent before God is to not pretend that I am something before God. To be unpretentious is to stand in humility before God. I stand before God just as I am, with no attempt to justify myself before God. For, my justification would be fantasy—that is, nothing. It would be an attempt to show God what I have made of myself. It would show God that I have put my self as my sole concern. It would be to lose sight of my eternal aspect.

So it is more truthful to be humble before God, to be transparent, unpretentious, and to stand as one who no longer counts before God. Then I can truly turn toward God in self-denial and self-forgetfulness. This is not the denial of wanting to not be. This is not the forgetfulness of fanciful dreaminess. This is, rather, the self-denial and self-forgetfulness of love. To be humble before God is to be turned toward God. The only way of turning toward God that bridges the chasm between my self and God is to turn toward God in love.

To turn toward God in love is the self's stepping into the nothingness of itself. It is the nothingness that is the chasm between self and God. It is the nothingness that was opened up when I had to choose to be a self initially. I chose to be a self because this is the spirit's potentiality in freedom. In addition, I have to be in the world as this individual, and I have to choose, therefore, to be a self. Once chosen, however, then God appears before me, though separated by a chasm that I have to find a way to bridge. I have to bridge it because God is for the self the only way to its completion.

The usual way to bridge the chasm between my self and God is to create churches, dogmas of belief, and doctrinal liturgies and rituals. This is to create nothing but what Kierkegaard calls "Christendom." But then all that happens is that the self falls into the hypnotic obsession with the aesthetic approach to God, wanting to feel loved, cared for, protected, etc. Or the self may fall under the spell of the ethical, in which it is one's duty to love God, to worship God, and to join with others in praying to God. Existentially, one has, without knowing it, lost that very self that one had chosen or thought that one had chosen.

To truly bridge the chasm that exists between self and God, a chasm that is, after all, the self itself, is to begin with the self's awareness that it exists only before God. This means that only before God is the self aware of having chosen to be a self. Being aware of being a self before God is to be aware of the separation between that self and God. This is to existentially know this separation as sin. To be separated from God is to feel existentially guilty and sinful. To realize one's existential sin is to feel humble before God, for one is still existing *before* God. To be humble before God is to be turned toward God, but not in fear of punishment, supplication for forgiveness, or anxiety about salvation. Rather, being turned toward God in humility is to be turned toward God in love. To be turned toward God in love is to be transparent before God, invisible to God because my focus is not on my self. Therefore, I stand before God in self-denial and self-forgetfulness. To stand thus before God is to no longer count as a self. To no longer count as a self before God is for the self to step into the chasm, to step into the nothingness that was opened up by the initial positing of the self. That is, it is to step into the nothingness that underlies the self. When the self steps into the chasm of nothingness, of empty separation from God, the chasm, the nothingness, the empty separation disappears. This is the final bridging of the chasm. The chasm itself disappears as the self surrenders itself in love to nothingness so that it can truly rest in God. When the self, which is the origin of the chasm of separation from God, which is the chasm itself, steps into the chasm, it steps into its own nothingness. Both it and the chasm disappear, and only God remains.

This is Christianity for Kierkegaard. This is Christ's message through Christ existentially offering himself as the example. This is the existential meaning of what Christ did on the cross as he surrendered his very self, willingly entered the abyss, and gave himself totally over to God, to return absolutely to God. This is the first part of Kierkegaard's existential theology.

Return to the Single Individual

In *The Point of View* (Kierkegaard 1851/1998), Kierkegaard reiterates what his primary concern has always been, namely, what it means to be a self. It means first and always to be a single individual: "this matter of the single individual is the most decisive" (114). But he does not speak of the single individual in a general way, as an abstract category for philosophical discussion. He means the single individual existentially standing before God, the single individual who recognizes that he exists *only* before God, because to exist is to recognize that one's temporal being is nothing if there is not also the eternal aspect of existing as a self. The eternal aspect of the self is God. Therefore, to exist is to exist as a self before God.

As we have seen, however, to stand before God is to be in sin, and to be in sin in the awareness that one is in sin before God is to be humble before God. If we are not aware of being in sin before God, we will only know that we are anxious as a self. But if we are aware that there is a distance between the self and God, because we stand *before* God, then we will know that there is a nothingness between us. If we examine ourselves more closely, we will see that we are in sin because we stand in that nothingness which is the separation between the self and God. When we see that the self itself is this nothingness, then we are humbled before God.

Existing before God is to exist with awareness of the eternal aspect of the self. The self sees the eternal within it when it stands in relation to itself. The self is aware of itself; it has chosen itself, and it recognizes that this ability to relate itself to itself is because the self has something eternal in itself. The eternal is that which has always existed but it must be understood subjectively—that is, through the self's relation to itself. Then the self in relation to itself is, as we have seen, in relation to God.

The self who turns to God in love stands before God in self-denial and self-forgetfulness. The self forgets itself in its love for God, as Kierkegaard points out that Christ exemplified (*Works of Love*, 111). As the self enters the nothingness that separates itself from God, because the self has come to love only God and therefore comes to forget itself, the self in effect gives itself to God out of love. The self's love of God becomes the self's love *from* God because, as Kierkegaard says, "in self denial … every human being can come to know that he … is loved by God" (364).

This leads to a "second existence," since the first was surrendered to God in love. This second existence is the self's "existing in God" (117). When we come to exist in God, when we have stepped into the chasm that separated the self from God, when we have given ourselves to God, then we have a second existence. It is this second existence that Kierkegaard refers to as "the single individual." When we come to rest in God by virtue of having surrendered the self in love for the sake of atoning for our original sin of separation caused by our choice to be a self, when we give up that very self that we had chosen, give it up for the love of God who appeared before us when we made that original choice, then we come to rest in God. We come to exist in God. It is then that God, out of love for us, a love that returns to us by virtue of our love for God, bestows upon us a second existence. In the manner of Christ's resurrection, after he surrendered himself on the cross to God for the love of God, we too are resurrected as "the single individual."

This is the second part of Kierkegaard's theology. Where we started out as individuals who existentially realize that we have chosen to be a self, we realize that the only way to be a self is to be as this single individual self. But in our original choice, as soon as we made that choice to be a self, as soon as we chose the self, we found ourselves standing before God, as this single individual self that we chose to be. This original single individual self stood before God, and in anxiety stood before God because in anxiety we stood separated from God, our eternal aspect. In truth we had to willingly, and in love, surrender this single individual self who stood anxiously in sin before God, the sin that was the sin of being separated from God. We surrendered this self because of having come to the faith that in love we could bridge the separation. But we could do this only by totally giving over this single individual self to God. In surrendering this self, we came to rest in God. Then out of God's love for us we are given a second existence as this single individual self. But this second existence, this new single individual self, is now with God and in God, and not standing alone and anxious before God. This second existence is as a full self, restored to us because we first surrendered it in love to God. We are restored as a full self because this is what God is: the self in its eternal aspect.

Summary

Kierkegaard's position from the beginning was based in the only reality that really is. It was to stand as an individual fully aware of existing in the world. This is our true existential reality. We exist, and we exist as individuals in the world. We are not manifestations of any objective overarching reality, such as what the great systems represent, whether religious, political, philosophical, or social. When we take a stand in the way that Kierkegaard did, in and as our own existing individual beings, we necessarily find ourselves thinking in a new way. We are not trying to understand ourselves within the framework of a system. We are, rather, trying to understand ourselves as existing beings. For we humans, to be aware of our existing individual beings is to be aware of being a self. We see that we are not simply another form of life existing temporally, here today and gone tomorrow. In being aware of our individual existence, in being aware of being a self, we see that inherent in being a self is some kind of timeless aspect. This timeless aspect is what Kierkegaard calls the eternal aspect of the self. In some way we partake of the eternal.

The only word that we have for the eternal, a word that means something to the self, is "God." Since the word "God" has significance for the self, the word becomes a name, and the name becomes a relation. Thus it is that we find ourselves in a relation with ourselves through that which is eternal, God. When this relation begins, we feel all the anxiety of it because we feel so cut off and alone from ourselves, from this eternal aspect of ourselves. We are strangers to ourselves because we do not understand this eternal aspect of ourselves. Our anxiety before this aspect, before God, is the anxiety of guilt. We feel guilty, and this makes us feel sinful. Our sin is that we are imperfect in our existential self. We are imperfect because we are ignorant of that which would make us perfect in being. We are ignorant of that because we are separated from God, the source of perfect being. Thus, our sin lies in this existential separation from God.

Our whole existential reality then becomes concerned with finding a way to bridge this chasm between our finite self and our infinite self, God. In order to do this, we must come to love ourselves. In loving ourselves, we find that this is actually the infinite self that is living in us. It is our infinite self that is extending love toward our finite self. Thus, we feel loved by God, and in this way God is love as John said (1 John 4:8). Since the infinite and eternal aspect of the self is God's love, the finite and temporal self who was the anxious one turns toward its own eternal and infinite aspect. It turns toward God. The finite and temporal self gives itself over to this infinite and eternal aspect of itself, God. Then, having surrendered the finite and temporal to the infinite and eternal, the self rests in its infinite and eternal aspect. It comes to rest in God. This self realizes that it is still this single individual, but it is a transformed self. Its first existence, fraught with anxiety, becomes its second existence, now steeped in love.

PART 2

THE EXISTENTIAL SELF

Chapter 8
FROM KNOWING TO IGNORANCE

Recapitulation

We saw in the first part that Kierkegaard realized that the self can become a self only when it relates to itself in its eternal validity. This means that the self must see itself as a synthesis of the finite and the infinite, the temporal and the eternal, and freedom and necessity. The self first chooses itself in freedom, and this choosing of itself is its eternal aspect. The freedom to choose and the choosing must occur in the same moment. They can only occur in the same moment. Kierkegaard saw that the self's choosing itself presupposed that the chosen preexists in the chooser. In other words, in order for the self to choose itself, there must be a preexisting self who can choose itself, and there must be a preexisting self to be chosen. Thus, the self is not the originator of itself but is only the moment of freedom in which the self is aware of coming into being through the choice.

But its coming into being is not *ex nihilo*. If it were, then the self would be the creator of itself. Rather, the self's coming into being through choosing itself is the self's awareness of its existence, of its preexistence—that is, existing prior to the moment of its choosing itself. Thus, the self's choosing itself is more a becoming aware that it already exists. It is then that the self realizes that it *must* choose itself (necessity) though at the same time it realizes that it is free *not* to choose itself (freedom). This is the synthesis that comprises the self: since it already *is*, it can only choose what *is* already. But it must be chosen freely if it is chosen at all, because it is the freedom aspect that brings what is necessary into existence. Thus, in choosing itself the self chooses itself in freedom, and because of its already existing prior to the choice, it chooses itself in its eternal aspect. This is the self's eternal aspect: in the immediacy of the moment to freely choose that which is outside of the moment, outside of time. For the existing self, then, there is paradoxically only the moment, but the moment stretches into eternity.

The self is a self only when it realizes its eternal validity— that is, when in choosing itself it sees that it already is present to itself and has always been latently present. Being latently present, the self is always a potential existence, not yet fully manifest in the world, but already in existence in the spiritual sense. This is the meaning of Kierkegaard's convoluted opening paragraph of *The Sickness unto Death*, and it is worth quoting to see the sense of it.

> A human being is spirit. But what is spirit? Spirit is the self. But what is the self? The self is a relation that relates itself to itself or is the relation's relating itself to itself in the relation; the self is not the relation but is the relation's relating itself to itself. (13)

In relating itself to itself, the self is simultaneously the relating and the relation. This is another way of Kierkegaard saying that the self is irreducible. Its existence is self-evident. It is eternal in the sense of being timeless. The self's existence lies outside of time. This is what it means for the self to realize that it is spirit.

With this realization, the self also realizes that "there is a God and that 'he,' he himself, his self, exists before this God" (*The Sickness unto Death*, 27). "Before" means that the self exists "in front of" or "in the presence of" God. The depth of self-knowledge that is entered when the self realizes itself as spirit, in its eternal aspect, brings about this awareness of existing before God and the awareness of "rest[ing] transparently in God" (82). The self's awareness of itself brings, thus, the self's awareness of God as its source, and the self's choosing of itself is simultaneously the self's choosing itself before God.

In *Philosophical Fragments*, Kierkegaard states his realization that such "self-knowledge is God-knowledge" (11), and that with the self's awareness of itself there comes the thought that "since he himself is, God is" (20). Kierkegaard thus takes the self to the point of making a new choice, namely the choice for "having God as the criterion" for the self (*The Sickness unto Death*, 79). "This self is no longer the merely human self but is what I ... would call the theological self, the self directly before God" (79).

This is where Kierkegaard leaves the self, resting transparently in a God who has been chosen by the self as the self's sole criterion for itself; that is, "that directly before which it is a self" (79). In effect, then, Kierkegaard seems to have exhausted his original intent, stated in his *Journals*, as "to find the idea for which I can live and die" (Dru 1958, 44). This "idea" is apparently the faith "that the self in being itself and in willing to be itself rests transparently in God" (*The Sickness unto Death*, 82).

It would seem, then, that this is the end of Kierkegaard's excursion into becoming "that single individual," a theme that runs throughout his writings (Dru 1958). It appears, however, at least based on the earliest entries in Kierkegaard's *Journals*, that he had always presupposed God as both the cause and the justification of the individual's existence in general, and of his existence in the concrete particular. But although the appeal to God appears at some point in all his writings, in the first seven of Kierkegaard's works, the self is examined from a more philosophical and psychological view than from the later theological standpoint. These seven works include *Either/Or, Fear and Trembling, Repetition, The Concept of Anxiety, Stages on Life's Way, Philosophical Fragments,* and the weighty *Concluding Unscientific Postscript to Philosophical Fragments.*

When considering Kierkegaard's lifelong invectives against measuring the individual by appeal to any system whatsoever—social, philosophical, political, or theological—the validity of his constant naming of God as the cause and justification of the individual can be questioned. Of course, Kierkegaard was a theological student, studying to be a pastor, so it is expected that his theology would be God-Christ centered, as indeed has been shown. Yet, it can be argued that he let go of the real existential self in favor of the theological self. At least, in his writings there is a frequent focus now on one and now on the other. In other words, Kierkegaard seemed full of ambivalence regarding the validity of the existential self.

The second part of this work is therefore devoted to studying the nature of the existential self that appeared mostly in Kierkegaard's first seven books prior to the increasing focus on the theological self. The overall shape of his existential philosophy, as it was originally centered on the self, or individual, will be examined. This second part is not meant to negate or refute Kierkegaard's eventual utter absorption in God with Christ as his model. It is meant, rather, as a continuation of what he left incomplete when he turned toward God as the basis of self.

Early in his writings, Kierkegaard took as his model of the single individual the person of Socrates. The whole of his master's dissertation, in fact, *The Concept of Irony*, contains a constant reference to Socrates. Socrates is referred to in other works as well. The major difference between Socrates and Christ for Kierkegaard is the fact that while Christ represents the human individual standing in relation to God, Socrates is the human individual standing in relation to his own existence. Thus, where Christ represents Kierkegaard's existential *theology* of the first part, Socrates is the personification of the existential *self* of this second part. It is this line of thought that Kierkegaard broke off from when he resumed his theological development. It is this line of thought that will now be examined in order to complete it as Kierkegaard might have.

Socratic Knowing

In *The Concept of Irony*, Kierkegaard borrows from Plato to say of Socrates that his existence is somehow linked to the unfolding of the idea (11). Thus, Kierkegaard sees in Plato's Socrates "an ideal significance far higher than the Xenophontic Socrates" (14). With Xenophon, according to Kierkegaard, Socrates is a caricature of the ideal Platonic version. "Instead of the good, we have the useful; instead of the beautiful, the utilitarian; instead of the true, the established" (25). But to find the ideal in Socrates is more a superimposition of what Plato gleaned from him than what Socrates himself believed. The irony Kierkegaard sees in Socrates is that, far from having any belief whatsoever about the topics he enjoyed inquiring into with others, Socrates approaches the topics in ignorance. The topics that he was interested in concerned the questions of what is the good life, what is the best way to live, what are the virtues, and how does one learn them. Socrates claimed that he did not know the answers to these questions, but he would like to know because he is not sure about what constitutes the good life. But Socrates does reveal to Kierkegaard at least one belief, and this is that in the search for wisdom, one is really concerned with taking care of the soul more than with attending to the body and its mere physical comfort (68).

This belief is present throughout the portrayal of Socrates in Plato's dialogues. The soul is the seat of true knowledge because only the soul can perceive things in their essential forms. But this form is not the same as the form perceived by the senses because all sensual perception belongs to the body. The perception of the soul is, on the other hand, the perception of essences. Since Socrates believes that philosophy is truly the love of wisdom, and since he feels a divine calling to search out true wisdom, he is searching for the knowledge of essences (38). Since the soul seeks release from the body so that it can return to the eternal, it does so through the search for true knowledge. True knowledge is the knowledge of virtue, and this involves the person's character (230). This, then, leads to the belief that only by knowing the truth about the virtues can we know the best way to live so as to move toward the freeing of the soul from the body.

Kierkegaard finds a unique meaning in the way Socrates is portrayed by Plato in the early dialogues, which are "closest to the historical view of Socrates" (30). The significance of these early dialogues is that Socrates approached the assumed knowledge that was professed by the Sophists from the ironic standpoint of his own professed ignorance. He claims ignorance in the face of the Sophists' claim to the kind of knowledge that is encompassed by the term "wisdom." Socrates's claim of ignorance is made ironic by the fact that while he approaches the Sophists from the expressed desire to learn the knowledge that the Sophists profess to have, in actuality Socrates is motivated by the unexpressed goal of proving them to be just as ignorant as he. Indeed, Socrates later confessed to this goal as his divine calling to expose the underlying ignorance of those who profess to be wise when in fact they are not wise (38).

The Sophists

In Kierkegaard's view, Socrates was involved in a vocation by which all profession of the knowledge of the virtues is reduced to nothing. The knowledge that is under attack by Socrates is the knowledge of the individual virtues that the Sophists claimed to be able to teach. Kierkegaard believes that it is the Sophists who first began the kind of reflection that Socrates is known for (201). This is not mere thinking about *things*, such as the previous natural philosophers did. But, rather, the Sophists were interested in helping individual Greeks to learn how to become better citizens by excelling in public life (203). Thus, the Sophists were concerned with conduct, and by reflecting on how to live so as to best serve the state, they were essentially concerned with virtue. For virtue was thought of as excellence in action, and if the action was manifested in public life, then a certain set of criteria guided this action.

According to Kierkegaard, the Sophists turned the focus of philosophy from the *object* of speculation, such as the origin of the cosmos, how it functions, what are the first principles, etc., to the speculator himself, the individual philosopher, the *subject* (205). That is, the subject, the individual who does the speculation, now became the object of speculation. One of the underlying premises of the Athenians in the time of Socrates and the Sophists is that everyone should participate in the running of the state. This means that an individual's identity was connected to the degree of influence one had with others who together comprised the state. The Sophists claimed to be able to teach individuals how to have the greatest influence over others and to persuade others to one's own views. This attitude inevitably involves the virtues, for it is in the exercise of the virtues that individuals claimed to be more excellent than their peers. Thus, the focus on the individual, the subject, became a focus on how influential the individual was, and this in turn was the focus on the virtues, or excellence in action.

The Sophists emerged from the ancient Greek philosophers who wove so many diverse theories of the cosmos that it became confusing for many later Greek thinkers. The Sophists looked at everything that ancients had taught and concluded two things: the first, summed up in Protagoras, is that everything is true. The second, summarized in Gorgias, is that what is true is what we believe is true. Protagoras professed to be able to teach men how to develop virtuous characters, while Gorgias claimed to teach men how to excel in rhetoric, to be virtuous orators, and to convince others of the truth through the use of speech. The truth for both of these major Sophists was thus relegated to the relativism of who was the better persuader. There was, however, no clear understanding or knowledge of what was being taught, namely the specific virtues, on the one hand, and on the other, the value and worth of teaching persuasive rhetoric. What resulted, then, was a pure relativity of values and therefore of the understanding of what is the best way to live. Such statements as "man is the measure of all things" and "might makes right" sum up the essence of the Sophists' teachings.

The Socratic Reaction to the Sophists

It is no wonder that the Athenian state saw Socrates as just another Sophist, for he indeed looked like one by virtue of the nature of his activity (*The Concept of Irony*, 201). Kierkegaard points out that though the Sophists claimed knowledge of the ideas of the virtues they taught, in reality the ideas were just a profusion of thoughts with no coherency to them (147). Socrates, on the other hand, was searching for the clarification of the ideas in his questioning of the Sophists but ended up in pulling their thoughts down into the emptiness of his own ignorance. The Sophists' ideas were shown to be abstractions that were empty of real content or clear knowledge. However, the emptiness of the Sophists and that of Socrates revealed two meanings. Socrates showed the Sophists that they did not really know what their ideas meant. They had no real knowledge of what they professed, namely the virtues. The ideas were empty of content. They were simply thoughts on the order of opinions or beliefs and had only a vague relevance for the real world. On the other hand, the emptiness that Socrates brought to bear as his own ignorance revealed that the ideas were irreducible to mere thought. That is, no thought could define fully and essentially what these ideas represented. Even though the ideas obviously meant something, no one could say in any definitive way what they really meant.

As one result, the Sophists made the mistake of thinking that the ideas of the several virtues could be defined in an adequate way by associating them with specific situations in which the various virtues seem to appear. Thus, they ended up believing and teaching that almost any thought could fill in the content of the idea of any given virtue. As a second result, the Athenians thought that Socrates was claiming that the ideas representing the Greek values were really useless concepts that were totally without any meaning whatsoever. Thus, the Athenians came to see Socrates as the enemy of the people, who they believed were being better served by the Sophists.

Socratic Ignorance

Kierkegaard saw Socrates, then, as representing a principle that makes of real philosophy an actual way of life (180–81).

For, Socrates was not only professing ignorance, emptiness of knowledge, in order to entice others into conversations. He was actually living from within his ignorance. That is, in his endeavor to find out what others knew about what they professed, Socrates did not approach them as already having the clear understanding within himself. He really did not know. In his effort to live well, he tried to live with virtue and to follow his own maxims: the need for continual self-examination; the idea that virtue is knowledge; and the belief that no one does evil intentionally. Paradoxically, in Kierkegaard's view, if Socrates had approached the Sophists with a presumption of already possessing or knowing the true essences, then he would have been deserving of Aristophanes's characterization of him (145), for he would have lived ostentatiously.

While desirous of the knowledge of true virtue, Socrates was not dependent upon its achievement for living a virtuous life himself. It was because of truly being ignorant of this kind of knowledge that Socrates could actually be courageous, just, temperate, and wise. That is, it was because of, and not in spite of, being truly ignorant that Socrates manifested courage in exploring his own and others' soul or mind. He was also able to treat all people equally and show justice in his interactions with everyone, aristocrat or plebeian, statesman or craftsman, because he never knew from whom true knowledge would come. He was motivated to practice temperance because physical comfort was never as real or as character shaping as the inner work of searching for wisdom. And finally, Socrates was wise insofar as he acknowledged that he had no wisdom whatsoever, at least as defined as a clear knowledge and understanding of what made for a good life, real happiness, and a worthy character.

Being actually ignorant of knowledge of the only things that mattered for him—that is, the virtues—and yet being enthusiastic about searching for such knowledge gave Socrates the appearance of already having the knowledge he was seeking. This gave his interactions with others the quality of irony—that is, appearing as already knowing what he was questioning others about. In fact, the real ironic aspect of Socrates was his ability to live virtuously without having the slightest thought of what the idea of the virtue meant. He thus lived in emptiness in that there was no content of knowledge that motivated him. He knew how to live but did not know what he knew. It was specifically due to his ignorance that the right and true way of life could manifest itself in Socrates's daily activities.

Kierkegaard explains how this was possible with the realization that because of Socrates's ignorance, nothing is able to retain its absolute validity (196). In his ignorance, Socrates is actually standing in the soul's emptiness, that to which he reduced all knowledge. Just as Socrates showed the emptiness of all Sophists' knowledge, so he showed the nothingness of the soul. For, as Kierkegaard says, "in order to become really congruent with its object the soul in its cognitive activity must become nothing to the same degree" (68). Socrates did not profess ignorance while secretly believing in anything that would support him in this nothingness. Socrates's life was, rather, a continual revelation to others of the way that a soul that dwells in its own nothingness can nevertheless reach the idea of the good, the beautiful, and the true. It does this by seeing in the ideas not the goal of knowledge, not the sought for object of knowledge, but rather negatively, as the absolute boundary of knowledge (197).

We have thus traced the significance of Socrates for Kierkegaard. We have gone from Socrates the inquirer, the seeker of wisdom, to Socrates the wise. The knowledge that constituted wisdom for Socrates began with a search for the true definitions of the ideas of the virtues that the Sophists taught. It will be recalled that the idea of virtue for the Greeks was connected to the idea of excellence (*arete*) in some activity or skill. Since no positive knowledge could be gained about what the virtues really were, the knowledge that Socrates acquired that made him wise was that he knew nothing, and no one else did either. The virtues could not be defined adequately, and yet the ideas of them had real meaning. They indeed continued to mean excellence, but with the Sophists and Socrates the virtues were associated with character. Thus, they came to mean excellence of character.

One aspect of the irony of Socrates was that, for Kierkegaard, the use of reason to get to the essence of the ideas led only to the negation of each definition as it came up. Though reason led to a professed clear conception of the idea in the later Plato, for Socrates reason only led to the realization that no thought could express such essences. Reason is a method of thinking, and thinking is a means to knowledge. But knowledge, for Socrates, is recollection by the soul of what it already knew but has forgotten that it knew (70). But when knowledge is concentrated in definitions, then reasoned thinking will always be able to find an exception to the definition.

Socrates brought his own soul's recollection of the true knowledge of virtue to bear upon the reasoned and colloquial knowledge of the Sophists. The knowledge that Socrates brought out to negate the Sophists' knowledge was the soul's recollection of the true knowledge of the virtues that inhered in the soul. The essence of the virtues resided in the soul but could not be expressed fully through any thought or word. The virtues could only be manifested through action. The soul reveals its knowledge, then, not as conceptual thought that uses words, but as action. The soul's own essence, then, is the inherent knowledge of how best to live.

Kierkegaard is using the same approach as Socrates to arrive at an understanding of that which cannot be put into words and expressed as conceptual understanding. Though we can act as if we understood what the virtues are and what the best way to live is, when pressed we can no more adequately explain our understanding through conceptual thinking than could the Sophists. As Socrates did, we must acknowledge our ignorance. Being ignorant we stand upon emptiness, for our supposed knowledge is really empty of content. This emptiness is the soul's own nothingness. The soul knows that there is the absolute, but just what it is cannot be defined. Though it has this knowledge that there is the absolute, what it sees when it looks for it is nothing. This is the irony, that where the soul is sure there is something, what it sees is nothing (77).

The real Socrates, for Kierkegaard, is the one whose actual way of life is a constant alternation between what is represented by life and death. "The soul is the life principle" (74). In the general Greek conception, the soul is set free from the body upon the body's death. Socrates's main concern is for the soul, as we have seen. Thus, paradoxically, in order to care for the soul, he must also care for the body as long as it is alive. But, insofar as the philosopher lived primarily in the soul, the ideal is always that it be set free from the body, which always drags it down. So Socrates was always pondering death and preparing for it (76). He was, however, as comfortable thinking that death was a setting free of the soul as thinking that death was an absolute ending of everything, soul included (82). In other words, Socrates faced the infinitely real and the infinitely nothing with equal composure (81). The irony of Socrates is seen in its essential form when Socrates applies his ignorance even to death. Where most others would quake in fear of death, Kierkegaard sees in Socrates's ironic ignorance about death another bit of inherent knowledge in the soul. Though there is absolutely no way to prove, disprove, argue about, or otherwise define what is meant, the soul seems to know that nothing bad can happen to a good man in life or in death. That he is certain of his goodness seems to be implied in his overall attitude toward any of the possible conjectures of the nature of death (78). He is certain of his goodness because all along Socrates has tried to take care for his soul, and the soul has true knowledge of how to live in the best way. Thus, in caring for the soul Socrates was actually allowing the soul to express itself as a virtuous life, even without being able to define what that virtue is. Thus it was that he claimed to be ignorant of what virtue is. Caring for the soul was, then, based on Socrates's willingness to live within the soul's emptiness, that ignorance that he used to evaluate the knowledge that others claimed and that eventually took all others' knowledge into itself.

It is this nothingness revealed as the emptiness of knowledge and nothingness of the soul that is the precondition for the truth to emerge and for real virtue to be lived. Only when the individual stands in nothingness, free of the preconceptions that cause people to think they know when in fact they do not know, free of the defining thoughts that would in effect limit the limitless and finitize the infinite, only in such a state of emptiness can real knowledge emerge. But this real knowledge, the kind that constitutes wisdom, can only consist of the soul's moral action. The person who lives by this innate wisdom of the soul has realized the best way to live and the best way to achieve happiness. This is what Kierkegaard refers to as the irony of Socrates, and it is the true existential individual living by faith in the soul's innate wisdom, even as the individual proclaims ignorance of what it is that he has faith in.

Next we will follow the development of the existential individual as the unfolding of the soul's innate wisdom through the individual's taking a stand in nothingness. It is in nothingness that the individual as represented by Socrates is born. Kierkegaard explores what it means to be that individual, what it means to be a Socrates who is in constant interplay between the body and soul. In exploring this further, Kierkegaard uncovers what it means to live in truth, as revealed by the inwardness of Socratic wisdom, an inwardness that is the result of standing in the emptiness and nothingness of ignorance.

Chapter 9
BECOMING THE EXISTENTIAL INDIVIDUAL

In *Either/Or* Kierkegaard continues what Socrates had demonstrated with his way of life. Socrates had shown that we are always having to make a choice between living for the body or living for the soul. While care of the body is necessary for harmonious living, when it is treated as sufficient for happiness then we are likely to end in disappointment. So the care of the soul was held by Socrates to be the more important of the two, such that each individual who is reflectively living life realizes that life constantly presents us with the necessity of making the choice between serving the body with its concern for pleasure and comfort, or serving the soul with its concern for virtue and wisdom. Just as Socrates undertook his search for wisdom out of a sincere ignorance of what real virtue and wisdom are, so too do we always stand in the emptiness of ignorance when it comes to making our choices in life. The paradox is that we cannot avoid living life in ignorance of the best choices to make, whether any given choice is made out of concern for the body or concern for the soul. Life is for us, as it was for the Greeks, an apparent guessing game, with doubt and uncertainty the only basis for playing it. One is asked to make the correct choice, but one has no real knowledge as a basis for making the right choice. So the question we are always facing is "either/or," choose right now.

The Aesthetic

The easiest choice to make in life is for the body, what Kierkegaard calls the aesthetic. It requires nothing but choosing the most immediately accessible object that will bring pleasure. In *Either/Or*, volume I, the individual, Victor Eremita, reflects that when we try to live life with some degree of awareness or reflection, the first aspect we become aware of is desire. He has many desires, "sometimes ... trivial ... sometimes ... exalted, but they are equally imbued with the soul's momentary passion" (26). Desires are momentary passions that can easily become obsessions with their sole objective being to bring pleasure to one's life. Once a desire takes hold of us, our whole life seems to be centered upon finding the object that will best or most efficiently procure for us the fulfillment of pleasure.

The most immediate form of pleasure is when we passively enjoy the objects of pleasure, such as we do with music or the arts in general. Pleasure is always grounded in desire, and desire is ultimately for happiness. Thus, the underlying goal of pleasure is to awaken the soul to its happiness, which is to awaken it to the eternal, the absolute. The aesthetic pleasures found in music and art seek to instill in us the sense of harmony and the beautiful, two intimations of the eternal and absolute for the soul. In our passive receptivity to these sources of pleasure, the soul is reminded of its innate recognition of these two forms of the eternal and absolute, harmony and beauty. The passivity that is the basis of this easiest means of aesthetic pleasure is similar to the ignorance of not knowing, in that in both there is an emptiness waiting to be filled. But as we have seen with regard to ignorance, when the soul stands passively in its emptiness, then it can recollect what the eternal and absolute are. Thus, through the passive receptivity that is an aspect of ignorance, the aesthetic objects help the soul recollect its innate knowledge of beauty.

In Mozart's opera *Don Juan*, Kierkegaard sees the character of Don Juan as representing the eternal tragicomedy of human life, a theme that Kierkegaard examines as the aesthetic way of life (142–43). Sensual pleasure, which is joy, lust, the demands of passion, and the tempestuous flight of imaginings, awakens love within the soul, which is another innate recollection of the soul, another aspect of the soul's life that eludes definition (61). Awakening to love is different from awakening to beauty in that love involves an object that is not only loved but thereby becomes an object of desire, a desired object to possess. When beauty is awakened and aesthetically enjoyed through a passive reception of music and art, it tends to remain in the passive enjoyment. Love, on the other hand, while it begins with the same passive reception of beholding an object (other) who awakens love in the soul, moves the one who feels love toward that object, that other. Thus, love, being of the soul, has the element of eroticism that causes the lover to desire physical intimacy with the beloved. This is the sensuous element in the soul's life. Thus, though it is the soul that is the seat of love, because the soul is attached to the body, there is the physical element that can cause the love to become solely erotic in nature, such that the fulfillment of sexual pleasure becomes the main goal.

A person who gives himself over to the erotic becomes bound by the erotic passion. Such a person is driven from within by this passion, and because of the internal source, one can be misled into thinking that it is one's soul that is driving one. But one is in fact becoming a seducer, for the erotic is a passion, and as a passion it is a power, a force that drives one toward the object for the sake of possessing the object. Kierkegaard uses the image of Don Juan as an example of a person who, despite his erotic conquests, is only a power and not a true individual (*Either/Or*, 1, 105–06). He is, in fact, reminiscent of the Sophists, whose only interest was in persuading others of the rightness of their own views. The seducer is concerned only with having power over another, getting the other to comply with his wishes.

Though the erotically impassioned person may feel a sense of fulfillment such that he feels that he has become a true individual, he is an imaginary individual only. This is because for the erotically aesthetic person, the object of erotic desire is imaginary only. The seducer who is striving for the conquest of his beloved is motivated by the erotic passion, to be sure, but a passion that itself is fed by an image of the beloved, such that the real person is never allowed to become present. Kierkegaard presents this tragic outlook as the presentation of a seducer before an audience in a passage that begins with the words, "I give the daughter of sorrow a dowry of pain as a wedding gift. She is my creation," and ends with, "she constantly comes into existence only as I bring her forth" (151). The seducer himself is the source of the pain that he inflicts upon his creation. He is also the source of his own pain insofar as no sooner does he conquer, that is, seduce, his imaginary beloved in the flesh, than he plunges again into the abyss of nothingness as his image itself disappears into the void.

This is because the seducer "has his ideal, the content of his life, the fullness of his consciousness, the essence of his being, in some manner outside of himself. He is always absent, never present to himself" (220). One can only be present to oneself when one is in the present. But since a person is living in the imagination when enthralled with the erotic aestheticism, that person becomes absent once the imagination has been lived out in fantasy and results in temporary sensual satisfaction. The person is thrown once again into his own inner emptiness.

This, too, is reminiscent of Socratic ignorance in that when we do not have, or no longer have, what we were seeking, then we are thrown back into our inner emptiness. Socratic ignorance is the result of a lack of real knowledge, whereas realizing one's absence to oneself is the result of a lack of the imagined other. The parallel can be expressed in this way: emptiness is the inner state that results when we become aware of not knowing and not having that which we have imagined our existence to depend upon. Either desire, for knowledge or for the beloved object, when not attained or when proven to be illusory, can throw us into a void of meaninglessness. This is because such a person lives in either the past or the future. The result of living in the past is that a person is living in the memory of what once was. The person's whole meaning of life lies buried in some past event, which in the present is only a memory. But because the person dwells in the memory, the present is missed. Likewise, the result of living in the future is that one is living in the hope that the imagined object of desire will come one's way or that one will find it. Dwelling in the future through hope, one is again absent in the present.

The aesthetically oriented person is not yet an individual, for he is not present. He is not present to himself or to the world. He is not yet separated from the other. The life of this person is lived aesthetically, always engaged in the search for the next source of pleasure, and when this involves the erotic, as the aesthetic life eventually will, there is the continual search for the next object to seduce. And the person who is the beloved erotic image is not really a person to the seducer but only an object because that person is only an image in the mind of the aesthete. As a result, the beloved is also prevented from becoming a real individual in herself.

The aesthete also is but an image to himself. It is not that he *has* an image of himself, but that he *is* an image to himself. This is because his image is in the image of the object of his desire. To paraphrase Kierkegaard, he is real in the world only when he shows himself to the world through the object of his desire (*Either/Or*, 1, 311). Only when he sees himself reflected in the other whom he seduces can he feel real in the world. Only when the seducer makes the other into an extension of himself through the act of seduction can he feel that he is real, because he can then see himself in the world as an object in the other. But his existence achieved in this way is actually a nonexistence, for it is imaginary only, and even in the conquest of the other through seduction he is not real. For he does not relate to a real other, he does not recognize a real other, and therefore he does not stand as a real individual before the other. If he were to recognize the other as a real other, then he would stand a chance of being a real individual in himself. But, rather, he destroys the other by incorporating her real existence into his own imagined beloved. Thus, his own life is reduced to a mirror image, and even that is taken away when he removes the mirror, or, what comes to the same thing, when he takes himself away from the mirror.

Then the aesthete is eventually thrown into, or finds himself suddenly in, nothingness. He is nothing. His existence is nothing. He really loves nothing, for what he thought he loved has proven to be only his image of it. In the end he is nothing, because he really has nothing, and this condition is made absolute, because there is nothing more to lose (323). This is an inner void in which life becomes increasingly nothing more than a series of alternations between the past and the future, between memory and hope. There is nothing left to lose, because the individual has never become present to himself. What has never been cannot be lost. This is like

Socrates saying to the Athenian court that he cannot be guilty of teaching new doctrines, because he knows that he knows nothing and therefore has nothing to teach. The difference is that the aesthete is not reflective in this way. He makes no reference to himself. He makes reference to the erotic object of desire, to the next seduction, seeing himself only in the objectified other, but he makes no reference to himself, because he has never been present to himself.

However, the aesthete still has a soul, and this soul knows, if only in a secret and silent way, that in the erotic moment of pleasure all such "momentary enjoyment is, if not in a physical yet in a spiritual sense, a rape, and a rape is only an imagined enjoyment" (337). This secret reflection of the soul reveals two things. First, that as long as we breathe, the soul is always present, though not always present to itself. The soul can fall asleep in the imaginings of the erotic life, as if in a perpetual dream. Second, what is revealed is that if the soul is stirred into wakefulness even if for a moment, the soul immediately recognizes that it was hypnotically enthralled with the illusory and imaginary. It sees that the "very quintessence of the erotic ... (is) ... fear and trembling ... to the degree that it takes away ... self-possession" (343). Indeed, the person in his soul—that is, in his very core—recognizes that "I dissemble by day, at night I am sheer desire" (348). Then, in a revealing confession, the aesthete says, "if she yields to me, then she will save the interesting out of the shipwreck" (348).

The soul sees that it has become totally immersed in its imaginings. The whole situation is rather like the Sophists being convinced that they know when in fact they do not know what they think they know, and they do not even know *that*. This is the soul's enrapture with its imaginings. Just as the Sophists needed a Socrates to awaken them from their imaginings, so, too, the soul needs to be awakened from its dreamlike state. The only way for the aesthete to be awakened out of his imaginings is either for the beloved to announce herself as a real person, thereby forcing him to remove his images from her real person, or for the soul to awaken through insight into its essential emptiness and nonexistence. The two always lead into each other. In the first way of awakening, the beloved, as a real person, resists the persuasive power of the seducer, just as Socrates resisted the arguments of the Sophists, forcing the seducer to realize his essential emptiness, just as Socrates forced the Sophists to realize their essential ignorance. If, on the other hand, the soul awakens to its basic emptiness, it will release the beloved object, because it will see that where it thought there was something, in fact there was nothing. This is reflected in the Sophists' realization that where they thought they had knowledge, in fact they had no knowledge at all.

It is only by seeing the emptiness, meaninglessness, and nothingness of that with which we were infatuated that we can begin to be serious about our life. In being serious about our life, we begin to be present to ourselves. We are not present in the way of the aesthete who looked for immediate gratification while actually inwardly living in the past or future. Rather, we are present in a self-possessiveness that recalls oneself to oneself. In this way, by acknowledging the nothingness of all our efforts to locate ourselves in the world, we are forced to come to ourselves in our ignorance and to seriously take a stand in the world in all our ignorance. This is to be the kind of individual that Socrates was for Kierkegaard.

The Ethical

Throughout *The Concept of Irony*, Kierkegaard portrays Socrates as being concerned with one thing only, and that is to perseveringly investigate others who claim to be wise so as to discover what is true wisdom. Socrates is not ever convinced by any of those he questions that their "wisdom" is the true wisdom that he is seeking. Though he questions others and converses with others about the good, the beautiful, and the true, he always subjects their statements to the scrutiny of his own innate wisdom that in his soul is, as we have seen, the awareness of not knowing anything—that is, the awareness of being ignorant. From this awareness Socrates is then standing in the nothingness of his soul, thereby being open to freshly discovering what is *really* good, beautiful, and true.

In the second volume of *Either/Or*, Kierkegaard focuses on the individual whose soul has awakened to itself in the Socratic sense. In the section called "Equilibrium Between the Aesthetical and the Ethical in the Composition of Personality," Kierkegaard points out in the opening pages how the aesthete has made for himself a most enigmatic mask behind which he has hidden from the world. The pseudonymous writer says to the aesthete, "In fact you are nothing; you are merely a relation to others, and what you are you are by virtue of this relation" (*Either/Or*, 2, 163). What is being pointed out is that we must acknowledge that the something or someone that we have been pretending to be is in its essence a nothingness. Rather than spend our life trying to conquer the object, which is really our own imaginary object, we can "win what is the chief thing in life, win yourself, acquire your own self" (167).

Just as the person's soul was immersed in the imaginary, thereby shaping the person as a nonexisting aesthete, making the choice *for* oneself, choosing to *be* a self, will thereby awaken the soul from its slumbers into itself. The individual self begins to be an individual self when the soul chooses to be a self, though this choice is actually the soul's recognition of its essential nothingness. With this choice, the self begins to grow in the soul, but the self can only grow where there is a nothingness. This is why the soul must come into itself, which is to come into its nothingness. The soul is then immersed in itself, and this is the self. Once the soul has awakened out of the imaginary, then it knows that it cannot return there. Or, rather, it knows that it is likely to drift back into the imaginary if it does not continually make the choice for itself, for being a true individual self. To revert back would be to allow others to constitute the self, thereby losing the self (168).

Thus, the choice is continual. This is something that must be done again and again in order to completely break the spell by which the imagination held us slave to the object. Socrates too, in living out of himself, in fulfilling himself as the oracle ordained, had to repeatedly venture forth as himself, had to repeatedly choose to be himself, to be an individual self. Kierkegaard calls this the ethical, for this is the good that we must bring forth from ourselves, namely to be a self (229–30). To choose the self, to choose to be a self, is to choose it in an absolute sense, for it is the soul's choosing to be itself. The soul awakens to itself, which is to awaken to and in its nothingness, and then within that awareness it chooses to be what it is, thereby becoming a self (181). The soul's choosing to be itself can only be good, and since in choosing itself it becomes a self, to choose to be a self can only be good. Thus, the soul's innate wisdom of realizing its ignorance and emptiness can only be good.

Yet this awakening brings with it some degree of anxiety. For when the soul stands in its own emptiness and it chooses to be a self, this self, too, is as if conceived in emptiness, in nothingness. Yet, once chosen, the self must orient itself in the world in a way that is different from the aesthetical. The only alternative available to the self is the opposite of the aesthete. Where the aesthetic life lived for whatever pleasure could be gleaned from the world, the ethical life lives for the absolute, the universal, which is the good (230). In choosing to be a self, the person orients himself to the good as the universal. Kierkegaard says, "The ethical is the universal" (259), and when the self becomes a self from within the emptiness of the soul, it sees that in choosing to be, it is choosing the universal. The ethical as the good, and the universal becomes the new orientation for the soul. This is an orientation that emanates from within the soul itself, and that is, therefore, the soul's innate wisdom. This wisdom begins when the soul realizes itself as emptiness, which is actually the discovery of the emptiness of the world, insofar as the aesthetic soul looked to the world for its fullness only to find that the world is empty of real meaning. Then within this emptiness the soul discovers a fullness, which is the individual and spiritual fullness of choosing to be a self.

The soul arrives at its innate wisdom only as it chooses to be a self, *this* individual. Before it chooses to be a self, the soul is subject to the whims and fickleness of desire. It is easily turned this way and that by the force of personalities with whom it comes into contact. This is why Socrates came across so many people who were influenced by the personalities of the Sophists. They have not yet awakened to their own innate wisdom as has Socrates. But Socrates awakened to this only when he chose to be a self—that is, when his self was pointed out by the oracle as a self with a mission. The mission was to know himself as the wisest individual. Socrates chose to be this self, but in order to truly be this self he had to know his own ignorance, his own emptiness. This is the paradox that Kierkegaard finds so fascinating, that in order for Socrates to be the self that was indicated to him by the oracle, to be in fact the wisest of men, he had to stand within his own ignorance of what that wisdom was the oracle said he had. This was the only real knowledge that he possessed, namely that he knew nothing. Thus, the awareness of being empty and nothing is the first experience of being a real self.

In order for the soul to realize its own innate wisdom as the self, it must set its gaze upon something other than the previous whims of pleasure. The soul must look to uncovering its own innate wisdom, but it cannot discover it without searching for it as the universal, as did Socrates. This universal is the ethical and is concomitant with choosing to be a self. The self, then, *is* the wisdom of the soul, and as such it is itself the ethical. But still the self carries on the search for the universal. It does not yet know itself as that for which it seeks. But seek it must, for if it does not seek, then the self runs the risk of losing itself again as the soul sinks back into the immediacy of pleasure, thereby losing presence. Thus, the self seeks for the universal in the way that Socrates did, by searching for a clear understanding of the knowledge that lies inherent within the soul and that others claimed to know. Paradoxically, this forms the basis of real interaction between the self and others. Only in this way does the self come to see that the universal cannot be found in any external form. The universal is not an object as were the objects that were the sources of pleasure. Though the universal must be sought as an object, for that is what the ethical is about, the self will eventually come to see, as did Socrates, that when measured by the standard of one's own ignorance—that is, of inner emptiness—the universal will not be found as any *thing* that can be defined. The universal *is*, but not as an objectively defined reality. For all definitions lead directly back to the soul's own emptiness and nothingness. Yet, only within that emptiness and nothingness will the soul discover its own innate wisdom, which is the self. Thus, it is to this emptiness and nothingness that the self constantly reorients itself as it goes about its life in the world.

This inwardness is for Kierkegaard the essential nature of being a true individual self. As he stated in *The Concept of Irony*, the Socratic principle "to know yourself" meant for the Greeks to "separate yourself from the other" (177). The only way to do this is to go inward and to see that one is indeed separate from all others. Going inward and being a self are one and the same moment, for when Socrates went inward to know himself, only then did he appear as a self for the first time. In this inwardness, with the emergence of the self, there is also the recognition of ignorance, of emptiness, and of nothingness. The self, then, does not appear as a positive—that is, as an active self-determining agent acting in and on the world. It is, rather, only a reflectively inward self-awareness that issues from nothing, yet that innately knows that it is different from every other self. This was the significance of Socrates's endlessly seeking out others to question, so that in the end it was not knowledge that stood out, but rather it was Socrates the individual self who stood out from all others. His standing out, however, was made possible because inwardly he stood in nothing. There was only the self who could stand forth in the world, because there was no content in the self. If there was any content that could be called knowledge, then it would have been that knowledge that stood forth, and not the self. For, to have had content would have made the self into an object. But since the self stood in ignorance, emptiness, and nothingness, it was only the self that stood forth. This is what Socrates represented for Kierkegaard. He was the original existential self.

Now we will turn to examine the way that truth can emerge from this inward emptiness. That is, the soul's innate wisdom that continues to function in the world, but is not definable without making it into something other than what it is, leads to the only truth that *is*, and it emerges from the inward-dwelling self. The inward-dwelling self, by which the self is a self, and by which the soul knows its own emptiness, is the existential path to truth. The truth *is*, and by this is meant that it cannot be predicated. For as soon as it is predicated, it becomes an object. Thus, the existential truth is the subjective.

Chapter 10

THE SUBJECTIVE AND THE UNIVERSAL

Entering the Subjective

Kierkegaard uses certain terms in speaking about the self and the quest for wisdom, terms that describe both the conditions for the self to emerge and the way by which the self maintains its integrity in living in the world. These terms are "inwardness," "ignorance," and "subjectivity." In the movement toward the self one must, as Socrates did, separate oneself from others. The Sophists represented the conventional, the popular, and, without stating it as such, the culture of ancient Greece (*The Concept of Irony*, 202–03). In this sense, the Sophists represented the state, the collective society of the city-state of Athens.

Kierkegaard points out that the relation that Socrates had with the state is another of his ironies, for though he professed to care ultimately for the state, all his life's activities had him questioning the ideational foundations of the state (232–33). So, following the directive of the oracle to know himself, Socrates takes the first step in this direction, toward the self, both for himself and for the Greeks and Western culture in general. For, Kierkegaard states that "this self did not exist prior to Socrates" (177).

Socrates took the first step toward the existential self by turning from the natural identification with the collective state to an inward awareness of how he stood as a separated being. He saw that when he separated from the collective, he had nothing with which to replace the certitude of the collective identification. He saw that as a separate being, he was empty and that his soul felt as nothing. This inner reaction to a willful separation from one's identification with the collective culture can lead many to regret the action, and, out of fear and trembling, to return to the fold, so to speak. But Socrates used this inner reaction of seeing his ignorance, emptiness, and nothingness to see if indeed he could discover something within. He did this by bringing his inwardness with its ignorance to bear upon the representatives of the collective, the Sophists. Rather than judge himself from the standpoint of the collective standard, Socrates judged the collective standard from the standpoint of his inwardness, and in doing so he became a self.

Socrates became subjective in turning away from the objective. Inwardness is subjectivity. When it is based in ignorance, or emptiness, then inwardness causes a person to feel anxious. What had been a standing in certitude and collective values became a standing in ignorance and emptiness. Where one stood in the objective in that one could indeed find the truth and the absolute "out there" in objective reality, when one turns inward to separate from the other, one then becomes anxious as the familiar is distanced in the choice of being a self. This is simultaneously becoming subjective both in where one stands and what one sees there.

In Socrates's time as in Kierkegaard's, as well, of course, as in our own time, there is always the social pressure to conform to the conventional beliefs and values. Conformity offers security and safety in numbers, by the mere fact of belonging to a society. Such belonging, however, is based on acceptance by others of oneself, and by oneself of the conventional beliefs and values. When we are concerned with the sense of safety and security, we are concerned with maintaining the inner feeling of these. We naturally turn to others to see what we need to believe, value, and strive for in order to continue in our sense of safety and security. We also naturally shy away from being a real self because of this. For, when we separate ourselves from all others, we separate ourselves from our conventional place in the world. When we separate ourselves from this, we separate ourselves from the objective world. Thus, when we separate ourselves from others, we become subjective. When we become subjective we have turned inward, and we have an initial feeling of danger and insecurity, of anxiety, because we feel the initial shock of seeing that we are essentially empty inside.

Kierkegaard sees Athens as reacting to Socrates's way of life. They saw Socrates as living in a way that pulled all the values and presumed knowledge of the virtues that he investigated in the Sophists into his orb of ignorance. In doing so, Socrates pulled all knowledge that defined the values and virtues into nothingness (*The Concept of Irony*, 40). It was as if Socrates's personality was seen as a spiritual black hole that sucked into itself all social values and understandings of virtue that were the cultural norm.

It is not that Socrates did not believe in the truth of the conventional wisdom as taught and propagated by the Sophists. It is rather that Socrates did not believe their definition of what it was that they professed to teach. If they could not say exactly what it was that they taught, how could they have claimed to teach it? Nor did Socrates doubt the objective reality of virtue; he doubted, rather, the common understanding of what virtue really is. Socrates also did not approach his conversers from the standpoint of being a teacher, for he had no clear concept of his own about the nature or definition of virtue. Thus, Socrates was not claiming the supremacy of being subjective over being objective. He was simply putting forth something that was new and utterly strange for his time. He was taking the daring leap into selfhood. In relation to the conventional, collective, and objective dimensions of living in the Greek city-state of Athens, or in Kierkegaard's own city of Copenhagen, being a self, standing apart, being subjective, and coming from a position of ignorance and challenging others to show why one should believe in their understanding of virtue can be seen as challenging the validity of the whole community. Such a new development can be seen as the first human excursion into nihilism.

Kierkegaard moves toward a sympathetic understanding of Socrates when he says that "from the viewpoint of the state his offensive had to be considered most dangerous, as an attempt to suck its blood and reduce it to a shadow" (178). In other words, the state saw Socrates as accurately reflected in the charges brought against him, as introducing new gods, corrupting the youth, and making the weaker argument the stronger. They saw him only from the standpoint of his separating himself from them, claiming ignorance of things that were clearly believed in by most citizens, and putting all of these beliefs into doubt, because no one could adequately define what these things were in their objective reality. The state could not have seen that Socrates was introducing something new into human life, namely the individual self.

What it took to be this new kind of person is what, for Kierkegaard, makes Socrates a true hero in the Greek sense of that term (211). It took courage and a new kind of faith. It required courage to separate from the other, courage to look at the truth of oneself, courage to accept the ignorance and emptiness that one saw there, and courage to challenge others to do the same. It also took faith that one was not thereby becoming evil or mad by doing so. It took a faith in the reality of what one was becoming, a self. And it took a faith that in some way to be a self was more important and more urgent than being a citizen of Athens.

The Subjective Stance toward the Objective

Separation from the other, turning inward, recognition of ignorance, and making the subjective the standard of truth, as inaugurated by Socrates, were new developments for the Greeks. In his avowed ignorance, he did not have any new insights to offer his fellow citizens. He had no new teachings by which to augment or supplant his contemporary Greek culture as represented by the Sophists. He was not a reformer or a redeemer. Socrates was unique in the Greek world, unique for Kierkegaard, and remains unique in our age as well. The idea of being a self remains embedded in Socrates's life as a reminder of what being a self is and what is required to be one. The actuality of being a self rests first on not knowing any longer what is true or what to believe. Socrates did not know. In the process of inquiring of others to find out if and what they really knew, Socrates stumbled upon the essence of being a self. It was a reality that could not be defined any more than others could define the virtues they claimed to know so well and to teach. Being a self rested upon the very ignorance that motivated Socrates to embark on his mission. But the ignorance is not only a not knowing. It is also devoid of content, empty, and nothing that can be described or defined. Thus, being a self is to be an empty nothingness.

Yet, the self is something, though not in an objective way. Whereas for most people their identity came from their status in the culture or society in which they lived, for Socrates, his identity came from his activity in life. The culture had no place for such activity, for Socrates's activity consisted in encouraging others to separate from their culture of beliefs, values, and presumed knowledge. For Socrates, the way of being was to turn conventional being on its head. Rather than saying "I believe in the culture of Athens, therefore I am a part of it, and therefore I am," Socrates was saying, "I do not believe in the culture of Athens because I do not know what that culture really consists of, therefore I stand apart from it, and therefore I am." The self is rooted in emptiness and nothingness because it is not a new idea or virtue or value that is offered to augment or supplant existing ideas, virtues, or values. This is the great crux that for Kierkegaard makes Socrates an enigma.

There is nothing positive about being a self, positive in the sense of having a definite content, a reality that can be objectively defined. To be a self is, rather, a negative in Socrates for Kierkegaard (*The Concept of Irony*, 209). To stand in emptiness and nothingness is the sole precondition for being a self. All else follows from this. The way that Socrates found to maintain this stance was to continually interrogate both others and himself about clarifying exactly what is known and what could be known about the universal meanings of concepts that were classified under the unifying concept of virtue. Socrates did not doubt that such universals existed. He just doubted that there were any people who could define these universals in a clear and rational way. But it was precisely this activity of searching, challenging, and negating all proffered definitions that revealed the self that Socrates had become. This was itself his positive approach to the universal. The universal is real but not clearly known. Yet by acknowledging not knowing what it is, the soul manifests the quality of virtue in a universal way as a self. Being not known, it is not objective. Being not objective, but yet being real, it must be subjective. Being subjective, it is truly what *is*. Being true allows Socrates to say that it is also what is good (232).

Since being inward is to be subjective, the self that Socrates had become was formed in the moment of turning inward to subjectivity. Being subjective is not the way to uncovering the truth, nor is it the quality of truth. For Kierkegaard, in his understanding of Socrates, subjectivity *is* the truth (*Concluding Unscientific Postscript to Philosophical Fragments*, 204–05). The "truth" refers to clear and concise knowledge, and the knowledge in question is what it has always been for Socrates: the knowledge that he does not know. Yet in not knowing he was able to actually live the truth by being subjective, a self. The only way to live the truth is on the basis of not knowing, of emptiness. The self, then, *is* the truth, and it is subjective. When the self searches for a clear knowledge of the best way to live, when it searches from the standpoint of being subjective, when it searches as a self, then the soul's innate wisdom is allowed to come forth as the very living of this subjective self. The self lives according to this innate wisdom when it emerges from within the soul. This wisdom is allowed to come forth, because the self, standing in the subjective, stands in its own ignorance. And out of this ignorance the soul remembers what its true wisdom is. As Kierkegaard points out, for Socrates, all such knowing is recollecting (205).

It will be recalled that when the soul chooses to be a self it involves the sudden awareness that the natural, therefore the easiest, way of life, of pursuing pleasure, does not result in the contentment and happiness that the soul seeks. Since such a pursuit of pleasure is actually an orientation of the soul toward external objects, included in this awareness of dissatisfaction is the turning away from objects and toward the soul's own ignorance of not knowing how to be truly content and happy. When the soul accepts this as the truth of itself and decides to live from within this awareness, it has chosen to be a self. Therefore, the self has its origin and ground in this inner state of the soul's own emptiness and nothingness. By allowing this emptiness and nothingness to continue to be the ground of the self, and not endeavoring to fill it with preconceived, conventional, and collectively held "knowledge," the self actually lives out the very truth that the soul desires, namely how to live such that one is content and happy. The self finds itself living according to the innate wisdom of the soul, which has been allowed to emerge through recollection because one sought in ignorance. One could only seek in ignorance, because when one is subjective there is no objective content to be sought. If there were objective content to the self, then the self would not be subjective, thus would not be a self. The ignorance or emptiness, then, acts as a vacuum that pulls all accepted and conventional knowledge into itself, resulting in the emergence of true knowledge from out of that vacuum as the subjective self.

So, there is an objective and universal knowledge that is the true answer to the question of how best to live. But this objective and universal knowledge is actually subjective and individual, thus there cannot be any objective definition of the content of this knowledge. The self actualizes this knowledge in the manner of its living, implying thereby that the soul knows clearly how to live. But when the self tries to convey this knowledge in clear and concise objective language, the most that can be said is what it is not (*Philosophical Fragments*, 44).

Therefore, for Kierkegaard, the personality of Socrates, the existing and real person who confronted and challenged others, in reality lived out in his actions the very knowledge of which he claimed to have no knowledge (*The Concept of Irony*, 227). In Xenophon, Kierkegaard notes that Socrates is portrayed as attempting to offer platitudes and utilitarian advice about how to live best (25). This could be seen as Socrates's attempts to give conceptual form to an innate wisdom that he instinctively knew. Perhaps, given his full acknowledgement of ignorance, the indication of instinctive knowledge could be a vindication of his idea that all knowing was recollection.

In Plato, however, Kierkegaard sees Socrates portrayed as a personality who was aware of a mission that was like a divine calling. It was specifically his calling to go around Athens testing out which knowledge was real and which was only presumed to be real, thereby fulfilling his duty to Athens as its greatest benefactor (93–96). In doing so, he revealed an innate wisdom but claimed ignorance about what it really was. In his discussions, which were more like question-and-answer sessions, some of the questions Socrates asked seemed to presuppose some moral principle or other, such as that it is better to examine oneself than fault another, and that it is better to act from reason than from passion (82). In Xenophon's portrayal, Socrates has positive content that looks like an awareness of the truth about how to live in the best way, and even though it is stated concisely, there is no attempt to define clearly the concepts that are implied in the advice. In Plato's portrayal, however, this lack of conceptual knowledge is in the foreground with the positive ideas of how to live being incidental. In both of Socrates's "biographers," then, the subjective and the objective are presented as interplaying in the dialogues.

It is clear that with Socrates the universal is expressed, and can only be expressed as the subjective individual's actual living, but only when the individual stands in the ignorance and emptiness of not knowing. Likewise, the subjective, when situated in the inner emptiness of ignorance, will reveal through one's actions and way of living an innate wisdom about how to live in the best way. This innate wisdom can only be objective knowledge about universal principles, values, and virtues. But when we try to explain, define, or describe what they are, using the only tools we have to convey objective knowledge, namely reason and language, we always fall short of the goal. The individual knows how to live, because the individual is subjectively aware of this in his inwardness. But the same individual cannot objectively conceptualize this knowledge, because as the subjective he cannot have any content without making himself objective.

Socrates was a valid and valuable personality for Kierkegaard in that he caused those who thought they could objectively state what these things were, and therefore thought that they could legitimately teach this knowledge, to finally come round to admit that there were at least gaps in their knowledge. In the Sophists' inability to clearly define and give conceptual form to what they claimed to know, they were revealing that they did not really know it and that they could not state that knowledge even if they did. The subjective and the objective were irreconcilable.

For Kierkegaard, the importance and significance of Socrates lay in this manner of being an individual self. Because he separated himself from the other, he also separated the subjective from the objective. He thereby made a clear conceptual definition of innate knowledge impossible. This was the result of Socrates's choice to be a self. It was an inevitable development in two ways. First, Socrates was following the inscription on the temple of Delphi to "know yourself" (*The Concept of Irony*, 177) in a literal way. Socrates took it seriously, and when the oracle pronounced him to be the wisest of men, he undertook to examine himself by examining others. Second, in examining himself through examining others, Socrates in effect separated himself from the others, thereby standing out from the others, and thereby becoming the first self in human history, according to Kierkegaard. Socrates could not have embarked on his mission to discover who was really wise without becoming a self. But once he became a self, he made it impossible for wisdom to be conceptualized clearly, concisely, and consistently. Yet, this did not prevent Socrates from living his life according to wisdom. Perhaps the ability to clearly state in conceptual language what is the best way to live is not as important as being able to remain aware of one's true inwardness in order to instinctively be able to live according to this wisdom.

Since Socrates was held in such high esteem by Kierkegaard, it is curious why the *Philosophical Fragments* ends with the statement that it was a project that "indisputedly goes beyond the Socratic" (111). At some point Kierkegaard went from seeing Socrates as the first truly individual existing self to seeing him as having fallen short of truly knowing himself (37). Apparently, full self-knowledge lies beyond the Socratic form of self-knowing. How and why this change in Kierkegaard's assessment of Socrates came about will be the focus of the next chapter. It was a momentous change for Kierkegaard, because it took him from seeing Socrates as the first existential self to replacing him with Jesus as the first prototypical self.

Chapter 11

SOCRATES CONTRA JESUS

Socrates represents the eternal truth insofar as he reveals the essential emptiness of the soul when true knowledge is seen as deriving from within. That is, when Socrates began his life's mission of searching for wisdom because he knew that he had none, it was his inner state of ignorance, of emptiness, that became not only the motivation for the search, namely to fill the emptiness with real and true knowledge, but also turned out to be the end, or result, of the search. In other words, what Socrates showed to the world was that the highest wisdom for a human to attain is to realize that we have no wisdom at all (*The Concept of Irony*, 37). This is the paradoxical nature of truth, for Kierkegaard, when it becomes subjectively based—that is, when the truth is connected to existence (*Concluding Unscientific Postscript to Philosophical Fragments*, 205).

Existence means something only for the person who realizes it subjectively. Only the individual can be said to exist, and only the existing individual searches for truth. When the search turns inward, then what is discovered as the objective is the eternal, essential, and universal truth about human existence. This truth is grounded in ignorance—that is, emptiness. The seeker of truth cannot discover the objective truth as the identity of thought and being, as the speculative philosophers arrived at, because the seeker is an existing person. As existing, the person stands in the subjective, precluding the identity of thought and being, and making such objective knowledge impossible (196).

Existence is a standing out and apart from the other, as we have seen. Thus, an existing individual has no grounding in anything considered as "other." Therefore, the existing individual Socrates was correct to refuse to give any content whatsoever to his wisdom. Human wisdom, insofar as it is determined inwardly, is empty of all content but this: that human wisdom is rooted in emptiness. The emptiness that is the ground for the individual existing person is the only stance that can be taken in order for the seeking person to come to any decision about the best way to live as an individual existing self. Whereas, if the person attempts to give a conceptual content to the innate wisdom of the soul, attempts, for example, to say of any given act, "that is an act of justice (goodness, wisdom, etc.)," the person assumes that he has knowledge of what constitutes justice, goodness, and wisdom. In fact, the wisdom that he is attempting to conceptualize vanishes in the attempt. This is the paradox of true wisdom, that the objectively eternal and essential universal is known only by the subjectively existing individual who stands apart from the objective, and stands in the emptiness of the soul's ignorance. In other words, in order to know the true universal, one has to stand apart from it. In standing apart from it, one stands subjectively in one's own existence, and it is from within that stance that the objectively true can actually be lived.

Kierkegaard posits a developmental process that leads from the aesthetic to the ethical that we have considered. He also recognizes the development of the subjective from the ethical state of the soul. Now he brings in a new category that develops out of the subjective. This is the world-historical (159). The world-historical is the unique context of being an individual existing human being. Socrates entered the world-historical by virtue of bringing the eternal into his existence. But it was more by accident that he did so because he was essentially concerned with the subjectively ethical, an ethical that could be discovered only inwardly. This was actually a stance apart from any context whatsoever except that of trying to prove whether the oracle was speaking the truth when she pronounced Socrates to be the wisest of men. That he had an impact on world history was accidental in that it was more the effect of the Athenian court than any conscious design of Socrates. He had no concern with entering world history. He was simply following his soul's inner promptings to discover if wisdom could be found in the world through others.

It is another paradox, because when we become individual existing human beings, we separate ourselves from the other, from the object, and therefore from the objective world. We inwardly separate ourselves from all that, because this is what choosing to be a self entails. Yet, when we stand in subjectivity and know that as the truth, then this means that the subjective is paradoxically the objective truth, because it is the universally objective fact that being subjective is the eternal state of human being. This means that the eternal and essential truth has become manifested in each and every individual existing human being. The eternal and essential truth entering into human existence gives a twofold picture. First, the truth is empty of all conceptual content, because it resides in the existing human individual. Second, the truth thereby enters the world-historical, because our human existence is in the temporal. The eternal enters the temporal in and as the individual existing human being.

The entrance of Socrates into world history was not sufficient for Kierkegaard, however. It was not sufficient that this condition of the eternal entering individual human existence occurred accidentally with Socrates. It was true that in Socrates's life his very manner of searching for wisdom was based on a choice that brought about his existing as an individual self. It was also true that when he took a stand in emptiness as his proclaimed ignorance he was revealing an eternal truth about the nature of the soul. Thus, it was also true that this eternal truth was intimately linked to his temporal existence. All this in itself was enough to have placed Socrates in world history. But it was his impact on the Athenians that actually put him into the world-historical (*The Concept of Irony*, 271). In other words, the objective conditions for the individual to enter into world history are meaningless without the subjective component. This subjective condition was met by Socrates because of the way he impacted his fellow Athenians. But it was accidental in that it was not part of the Socratic mission to have such an impact on others.

There is another world-historical individual who enters Kierkegaard's writings, and this is the person of Jesus. Where Socrates is paradoxical in the existential human sense, Jesus represents what Kierkegaard refers to as "the absolute paradox" (*Concluding Unscientific Postscript to Philosophical Fragments*, 217). This is because it is God as the totality of the infinite and eternal who comes to exist in the finite and temporal human individual Jesus. The issue that distinguishes these two in Kierkegaard's mind is that Socrates's entrance into world history was accidental and not an intrinsic part of his individual existing human being, whereas Jesus's entrance into world history was the deliberate design of the infinite eternal God.

To understand what this meant to Kierkegaard, we must examine it in depth. Socrates was a human teacher who was simply doing the god's will (*Philosophical Fragments*, 10). His responsibility was to bring others to the truth that they had within themselves, namely that they really know nothing despite the fact that they thought they did. Socrates exemplified this in his own life insofar as he began with ignorance in order to discover what was already in his own soul. But he did not define this and present it as his teachings as did the Sophists. Rather, Socrates continually tried to bring others to the realization that they themselves were ignorant of any real knowledge. At the same time he demonstrated for them that only by acknowledging their own inner ignorance and emptiness could they then access the true knowledge that their soul already possessed. This was for Socrates, in Kierkegaard's view of him, the "highest relation a human being can have to another" (10). But it is essential for the Socratic mission that the teacher does not try to teach pedagogically as did the Sophists. For this would be to actually take away from the student his own chance to recollect what he already knows. To teach in this manner would be to engage in another form of the seducer who we have seen before.

This was the essence of Socrates's teaching, and therefore of Socrates himself, as summarized by Kierkegaard. It is worth quoting in whole.

> This is how Socrates understood himself, and in his view this is how every human being must understand himself, and by virtue of that understanding he must understand his relation to the single individual, always with equal humility and with equal pride. For that purpose, Socrates had the courage and self-collectedness to be sufficient unto himself, but in his relations to others he also had the courage and self-collectedness to be merely an occasion even for the most stupid person (11).

But, adds Kierkegaard, what about our eternal happiness? What good is the knowledge we gain by struggling with ourselves to unlock the truth that we already possess? How does this lead to our eternal happiness? In fact, Kierkegaard continues, is not the precondition for discovering the inner truth that we first discover our untruth? (14). So, in being led Socratically to discovering what we already have in our souls, we must go through the region of our untruth, which is our emptiness, our ignorance, and which does not lead either way to our eternal happiness. What Kierkegaard seems to be saying is that since we have ignorance as the basis of our innate wisdom, it is impossible for this innate wisdom to result in our happiness.

Kierkegaard makes a sudden shift in his thinking by saying that in order that we learn the truth about ourselves, we must first discover what is not true about ourselves. By changing the words from the relation between ignorance and wisdom to that of the relation between untruth and truth, Kierkegaard goes on to say that it is God who alone gives us the condition for understanding the truth (15). Paradoxically, it is our existence as the single individual, which we are by virtue of separating ourselves from the other (thereby removing our content)—that is, both our truth and our untruth. It is this very existence that Kierkegaard implies as proving that we are created (15).

Kierkegaard has taken a sudden turn from the existential self of Socrates, who chose to be an individual self by taking a stand in ignorance, thereby in the emptiness of inwardness, toward the theological self created by God, who then provides the condition for understanding the truth and shows the truth. It is as if Kierkegaard asked himself, given that Socrates recognized his ignorance of having any knowledge of the truth whatsoever, and given that he dwelled in the emptiness of his soul insofar as it was ignorant, was it part of his soul's innate, though unaware, knowledge of the truth to conclude that he is in fact living in untruth? This would mean that the soul's innate wisdom includes the awareness of not only what is untrue but that it is untruth.

"But this state—to be untruth and to be that through one's own fault—what can we call it? Let us call it *sin*" (15). We made a choice to be a self. That choice included separation from the other and resulted in an awareness of ignorance of who and what we are and of the best way to live. This placed us in emptiness. Emptiness is bereft of any positive content at all, and thus is untruth. Living in untruth is existential anxiety, which is existential guilt, which in turn is sin. In *The Concept of Anxiety*, Kierkegaard made this clear when he stated, "a person seems to become guilty through anxiety about himself" (53). Then he states, "subjective anxiety is the anxiety that is posited in the individual and is the consequence of his sin" (56). Sin, then, is apparently due to the willful nature of choosing to be an individual self, thereby through our own fault choosing to live in untruth. But sin makes it possible to recognize God not only as the teacher, revealing the truth of our untruth, but also as a savior. For, Kierkegaard says, "What, then, should we call such a teacher who gives [us] the condition (for recognizing that we are in untruth) and along with it the truth? Let us call him a savior" (*Philosophical Fragments*, 17). To stand in emptiness, then, is to stand in untruth. To recognize that we are in untruth is to recognize the truth about our individual existence, namely that it is in sin that we exist. The truth, then, is that we are in sin through our own fault.

From this point on, Kierkegaard repeatedly offers us a choice of our own. Either we recognize the truth of who we are when we see in our innate wisdom that we are really outside the truth when we admit our ignorance, in which case we are in untruth, or we are left with only a Socratic explanation that we have expounded upon throughout this second part. The reason Kierkegaard went in this direction is apparently due to a confusion he noticed in the Socratic position. When Socrates asked his questions, he was helping the other person to arrive at the truth by himself through the power of his soul's own reasoning. In the moment of discovering the truth, the person discovered that he had "known the truth from eternity without knowing it" (13). To seek the truth is, then, impossible, for if it is a matter of already knowing it, then there is nothing to seek. It is only a matter of remembering what we already know. But it is also impossible to seek the truth if it is outside us, for we would not know what to seek. Therefore, concluded Kierkegaard, we stand outside of the truth, hence in untruth (13).

Thus, the paradox becomes clear. And it sounds much like the initial confession of Socrates that the only wisdom he has is that he knows that he does not have any wisdom. This new paradox is that, recognizing that we are in untruth is the sole condition for recognizing the truth about ourselves, namely that we are in untruth. But, where for Socrates the paradox lay in the fact that he was only trying to prove, or disprove, the oracle's pronouncement that he, Socrates, was the wisest of men, this new paradox is given to us by the appeal to the universal and eternal truth, which in its totality is God. Hereafter it is our relationship with God that becomes of primary importance for Kierkegaard and for our existential human individuality. What is needed is one more condition to be met, and that is for God to provide a means whereby we may be led to the truth of our untruth. Socrates cannot do this, for we have seen that he can bring us only to the point of realizing that we do not know the truth, and this is not the same as claiming that the truth is that we are untruth. He did not mean that we could not eventually know the truth.

But in the idea that we were in untruth there was the implicit implication that we could never come to the truth from within ourselves. In order to come to know the truth from our stance of untruth, we have to be taught it. The only one who can teach us the truth about ourselves is the one who possesses the full knowledge of human truth, and this is God (*Concluding Unscientific Postscript to Philosophical Fragments*, 141).

There must be a teacher like Socrates whose presence is essential to this knowledge. The only way that God can become present to the human individual is to take on human form. Where Socrates was the god's tool for awakening the individual to the truth of not knowing the truth, Jesus was God in human form sent to teach us what only God could teach, namely that which Socrates showed us we could not know by reason alone. Though this was not Socrates's positive teaching, this was the implication of his constant questioning and refuting what others professed. It is the absolute paradox that reason cannot reach but that underlies our human individual existence, namely, it is that "something that thought itself cannot think" (*Philosophical Fragments*, 37). This is to know what a human being is. It is to "have the criterion of truth, which all Greek philosophy *sought*, or *doubted*, or *postulated*, or *brought to fruition*" (38). It is the "unknown against which the understanding in its paradoxical passion collides and which even disturbs man and his self-knowledge" (39).

We cannot reason or otherwise think our way to this truth. We can only be directly taught it, but in such a way as we may see it existentially in another. We saw it existentially in Socrates in its negative form; that is, in ignorance. Kierkegaard wants to speak about the truth in its positive form; that is, as definite teachings. But for the absolute truth to have content, God needed to take on human form. The content then became clear, for it has always been about who and what we are. This is known only through faith (59). But unlike with Socrates, where the faith is in one's own ability to remember what one has always known, with Jesus the faith is in the teacher and his teaching, for it is the human form of God in the individual Jesus who is both the teacher and the teaching. Apparently, however, the teaching cannot be conveyed in thought any more than with Socrates it could be. For to convey the absolute truth about our human being, we have to see it existentially in the existential moment that the individual is.

It appears that Kierkegaard has brought up two domains of truth, neither of which can be conveyed through thought alone, and both of which needed their existential individual to demonstrate the truth in their existential being. For Socrates, the truth that he demonstrated is that we are ignorant of true knowledge of the matters that concern us most, namely how best to live. But this does not preclude us from being able to access the soul's innate wisdom that can remember what it knows. For Jesus, on the other hand, the truth that he demonstrated is that we live in untruth and in sin. As such we are forever precluded from directly knowing the truth of being. However, he, Jesus, has this direct knowledge, because he is from God and *is* God. Socrates therefore represented the first existential self, while Jesus represented the first theological self (*The Sickness unto Death*, 79).

In the next to last chapter, I will summarize what exactly Socrates meant to Kierkegaard. Despite Kierkegaard's turning toward Jesus and the theological self, Socrates maintained a special place in Kierkegaard's thought and spirit. It is almost as if Kierkegaard could not help being more deeply and existentially influenced by the example of Socrates than he was in relation to Jesus.

Chapter 12

KIERKEGAARD AND SOCRATES

Socrates was concerned with knowledge but not the speculative cosmological knowledge of nature that his predecessors were putting together. Rather, the kind of knowledge that Socrates sought was that which comprises wisdom. Kierkegaard looked closely at what Socrates called wisdom. He quotes Socrates as the latter stood before the Athenian court, saying, "What kind of wisdom do I mean? Human wisdom, I suppose. It seems that I really am wise in this limited sense" (*The Concept of Irony*, 170–71). Then Kierkegaard goes on to say of this human wisdom,

> The predicate "human" … is extremely significant. To be specific, when subjectivity by means of its negative power has broken the spell in which human life lay in the form of substantiality, when it has emancipated man from his relation to God just as it freed him from his relation to the state, then the first form in which this manifests itself is ignorance. The gods take flight, taking the fullness with them, and man remains as the form, as that which is to receive the fullness into itself,

but in the sphere of knowledge a situation such as this is correctly interpreted as ignorance. This ignorance is in turn quite consistently called human wisdom, because here man has come into his own right, but this right is precisely the right not to be merely man as such (171).

Without the relation to God or the gods to tell us who we are, what we are, and how we are to live, we are left to our own resources to answer these questions for ourselves. Our primary thinking ability is, of course, reason, but we must begin our reasoning from the standpoint of not knowing, of ignorance. In the quest for human wisdom, the starting point of ignorance is not knowing in advance, thus having no preconceptions of the knowledge we are seeking. This reveals not only that we are devoid of knowledge but also that we are empty beings without such knowledge.

It is implied throughout Kierkegaard's works that to *be* is to be defined in specific ways. To be defined is to have knowledge. Therefore, to have knowledge of ourselves is the only way by which we can be. To exist, on the one hand, is to experience oneself as being but without knowing the essence of being. Experience is thus differentiated from knowledge in the same way that existence is differentiated from essence (336). Being empty beings, and making knowledge a precondition of being, we can say that when we come into our own right as humans we enter into nonbeing. In this inner state of ignorance, emptiness, and nonbeing, it is up to us to think out for ourselves who we are, what we are, and how we are to best live. This is partly what Socrates undertook to do.

The essence of existing subjectively as individual human beings is that our lives become activity, defined more by what we do and how we live than by knowledge of who and what we are. Thus, Socrates did not bother with questions of our human nature or of the essence of human being. He did not bother about what we are. He apparently left that knowledge in the hands of the gods. His sole concern was how to live. This area of inquiry is open to us to think out without knowing anything about our objective place in the cosmos, how we came to be, and why. We may be able to speculate about such matters, but we cannot make ourselves into anything that such speculations may bring out in thought. The most we can do is to believe that we are such and so, but we can never know for sure if we indeed are that.

In the area of how best to live, however, we can arrive at definite knowledge and make ourselves into good persons. But we have to pursue this knowledge with an openness that, paradoxically, we have when we acknowledge with Socrates that we know nothing. This Socratic activity of searching for wisdom represented for Kierkegaard a heroic life, especially given the ironic outcome in which Socrates was able to manifest in his person all the virtues that define the good life. For, while he professed ignorance of what these virtues were in their essence, he was able to practice them because of his ignorance. He was able to say, for example, "since I don't know what death is, I don't know if it is something to fear or to welcome" (*The Concept of Irony*, 82). Thus, though Socrates could never discover an essential definition of the virtue of courage, for example, he was nevertheless able to manifest it in his attitude toward death based on his ignorance of not knowing.

This is the ultimate form of Socratic irony that Kierkegaard admired in Socrates, that not only in spite of his professed ignorance of the essence of the good and the true but also because of it, he was able to actualize these ideas in his life (197). Throughout Kierkegaard's study of Socrates, there is the interplay between the idea showing itself in Socrates and then again hiding itself in the interactions with his interlocutors. Kierkegaard says in this regard that "Socrates arrived at the idea but in such a way that no predicate disclosed or betrayed what it actually was" (137). Socrates, that is, arrived at the idea of virtue insofar as he lived it, but he could never arrive at the proper predicate or definition of it. He lived the good and the true; he lived the virtuous, without knowing what they were in their essence. The fact that Socrates was able to live in this ironic way suggests to Kierkegaard that Socrates knew without knowing that he knew, but knowing that he at least knew that he did not know (187).

It is this existential position of Socrates that makes him tremendously significant for Kierkegaard as the first truly individual self (177). As such, Socrates stood apart from all that had previously defined him, from the state and the official gods (168–69). In standing apart from the other he stood alone, empty of any positive identity, yet willing to examine himself and others in his quest for the true idea. He saw the idea that he was striving for knowledge of as a boundary (169). This boundary was for Socrates, in Kierkegaard's interpretation of him, the boundary of what we as humans can truly know. Yet, though the full knowledge of the idea may lie beyond the idea as held in the soul, nonetheless we all have, as Socrates had and urged others to recognize as having, the primary duty in life to strive for the knowledge of the idea. Though we may not be able to reach the full knowledge through reasoned thought alone, yet it seems possible to awaken our soul and its awareness to the influence of the idea upon our life, and thereby to live the good and true life even without knowing objectively what that is without being able to define it.

This is possible only when we stand as the existential self, as Socrates, acknowledging our true ignorance of the matters we previously claimed to know. Only when we stand as the existential self in the inward emptiness of our ignorance can we really begin to search for true wisdom. Only when we stand in the nonbeing or nothingness of our existence can we live life with the openness that allows us to face events in life without assuming that we know for sure if they are good or evil. This was Socrates's significance for Kierkegaard.

In those areas of knowledge that were left unanswered by Socrates, namely concerning who and what we are, Kierkegaard had to turn to another individual whose actual person and life showed us these answers. Socrates's person and life showed us how we can learn the best way to live the good and true life in this world. Kierkegaard looked to Jesus to show us who and what we are, and to urge us to return to that from which Socrates separated himself. But it was a justified separation, for in separating himself Socrates showed us what it is to be an existential individual self. Socrates also showed us that only as this existential individual are we free to seek out true wisdom, which is, after all, what a philosopher does.

In the final chapter, I will attempt to summarize the significance of this literary journey that is being completed. Kierkegaard was a complex personality, as I think is apparent the more he is discussed. In summary, however, the way in which he reconciled the two poles of his existence, which are represented by Socrates and Jesus, must be examined in order to have a deeper appreciation of Kierkegaard's complexity.

Chapter 13

THE RECONCILIATION

Kierkegaard had always been divided within himself, from his relationship with Regine to his relationship with God. As soon as he stepped into being "this individual" through his breakup with Regine, he began to detach from his goal of being a minister of the church. His engagement to Regine, the whole idea of marrying, and taking on the role of a minister of the church all symbolized for him the kind of safety, security, and certainty that Christendom had become. But that was just the problem, sensitized as he had become to "the system," as he called Hegel's philosophy. The whole of Christendom had come to feel too safe, too secure, and too certain to any longer have any sense of reality about it. It had become just another system that ironically could not support the individual. It could envelop and incorporate the individual, but it could not support the individual.

Kierkegaard spent his whole life trying to reconcile the human need for marrying with the spiritual need for being a "true individual." For he saw that one could approach God only as an individual. The church had become inimical to his need for a God-relationship, so he could only approach God in "fear and trembling" as "this individual." Marriage represented to him the highest form of human love but which could only approximate the love that God promises if only one has faith. But the kind of faith that was necessary to approach God, as expressed in *Fear and Trembling*, was nothing like the kind of faith needed for marriage, as Judge William spoke of in the "Or" part of *Either/Or*. Kierkegaard could paradoxically find within himself the first kind of faith but inwardly quaked at the second form of it.

Early on, Kierkegaard saw in Socrates the exemplar of the true individual whose whole life was full of irony. The ironic aspect of the life he represented for Kierkegaard was that one individual, by rejecting the collective, the social, and the conventional, in short, by rejecting the system, could arrive at the universal. Where the system could only incorporate and annihilate the individual as individual, it was ironically only in and as the individual that the universal could be expressed in the world. The universal that Socrates personified was the moral universal, the Good.

But Kierkegaard could not rest there. In *Philosophical Fragments* he brought Socrates's version of the universal truth into question by contrasting it with Jesus's version of it. Socrates approached truth from within, as a recollection, as a realization that we have forgotten but that still lies buried somewhere within. But Jesus, as Kierkegaard pointed out, brought a realization of truth that was revelatory. Revelation comes about through repetition rather than recollection. We repeat in our lives the necessary conditions for realizing the truth until we finally have the revelation of truth. The conditions that are repeatedly experienced result in the ultimate revelation that it is not merely the universal that is expressed in and as the individual, but it is the Absolute Universal, God, who is expressed in and as This Individual, Jesus.

Through this path, Kierkegaard came to realize that though Socrates represented what it is to be a true individual, a true self, it was Jesus who represented what it means to be *this* individual, *this* self. This realization was expressed finally in *The Sickness unto Death*, in which Kierkegaard revealed the extent of the division within himself. As a true self he saw that he stands before God, as any true self does. And in standing before God one is always standing in sin. Kierkegaard saw that there is only one self, only one individual who is not in sin before God, and this is Jesus. All other selves who stand before God are in separation from God. But Jesus alone is the one individual who *is* the true Absolute Universal, which is God.

Thus, in Kierkegaard's experience the existential self, which Socrates represented, and as Kierkegaard found himself to be ever since breaking his engagement with Regine, can only result in the individual standing in separation from God. Standing before God implies being separated from God. The only way Kierkegaard could bridge this gap was to be the individual who stands transparently before God. This is to take Jesus as the prototype of the theological self, which is to *be* this transparency before God. To stand transparently before God means to relate oneself to oneself, and to be willing to be oneself. This is Kierkegaard's definition of faith, and it is the only way to step out of the sinful state of standing before God as the existential self. For the existential self is always in sin before God since it is in separation from God. But to stand transparently before God is to stand in faith in God. And faith, for Kierkegaard, is the absurdity of the forgiveness of sins through God's love. It is God's love that brings Kierkegaard out of the state of sinful separation into the joy of the forgiveness of this separation.

This, then, brings Kierkegaard full circle from the day he forsook the human love of marriage. He broke with the possibility of finding fulfillment in human love, thereby separating himself from human love and at the same time seeing clearly just how infinitely far he was from the love of God. He became the existential individual seeking a true realization of Christian truth. The only way he could possibly compensate for the loss of Regine was to struggle toward the truly absurd, as represented by Abraham in *Fear and Trembling*. This ironic development in Kierkegaard led him to discover the true meaning of faith. In the end, perhaps he found that love that is higher than the human, that love which alone, so he saw, could forgive his original sin of having been born in a state of separation from God.

References

Capel, L. M. (1964). "Historical Introduction." In *The Concept of Irony*. Translated by Lee M. Capel. Bloomington, IN: Indiana University Press.

Collins, J. (1965). *The Mind of Kierkegaard*. Princeton, NJ: Princeton University Press.

Dru, A., trans. (1958). *The Journals of Kierkegaard*. New York: Harper and Row.

James, W. (1936). *The Varieties of Religious Experience*. New York: Modern Library. (Original work published 1902.)

Kierkegaard, S. (1841/1989). *The Concept of Irony*. Translated by Howard V. Hong and Edna H. Hong. Princeton, NJ: Princeton University Press.

_____ (1843/1990). *Eighteen Upbuilding Discourses*. Translated by Howard V. Hong and Edna H. Hong. Princeton, NJ: Princeton University Press.

_____ (1843/1944). *Either/Or*. 2 volumes. Translated by David F. Swenson and Lillian Marvin Swenson. Princeton NJ: Princeton University Press.

_____ (1843/1980). *Fear and Trembling*. Translated by Howard V. Hong and Edna H. Hong. Princeton, NJ: Princeton University Press.

_____ (1844/1980). *The Concept of Anxiety*. Translated by Reidar Thomte. Princeton, NJ: Princeton University Press.

_____ (1844/1985). *Philosophical Fragments*. Translated by Howard V. Hong and Edna H. Hong. Princeton, NJ: Princeton University Press.

_____ (1846/1992). *Concluding Unscientific Postscript to Philosophical Fragments*. Translated by Howard V. Hong and Edna H. Hong. Princeton, NJ: Princeton University Press.

_____ (1847/1995). *Works of Love*. Translated by Howard V. Hong and Edna H. Hong. Princeton, NJ: Princeton University Press.

_____ (1848/1940). *Christian Discourses*. Translated by Walter Lowrie. Princeton, NJ: Princeton University Press.

_____ (1849/1980). *The Sickness unto Death*. Translated by Howard V. Hong and Edna H. Hong. Princeton, NJ: Princeton University Press.

_____ (1851/1990). *Judge for Yourself!* Translated by Howard V. Hong and Edna H. Hong. Princeton, NJ: Princeton University Press.

_____ (1851/1998. *The Point of View*. Translated by Howard V. Hong and Edna H. Hong. Princeton, NJ: Princeton University Press.

_____ (1855/1944). *Attack upon "Christendom."* Translated by Walter Lowrie. Princeton, NJ: Princeton University Press.

Lowrie, W. (1970). *Kierkegaard*. 2 volumes. Gloucester, MA: Peter Smith.

Scofield, C. I., ed. *The Scofield Study Bible* (1996) New York: Oxford University Press. (Original edition published 1909.)

Underhill, E. (1995). *Mysticism*. London, UK: Bracken Books. (Original work published 1911.)

Index